The Quality Education
Challenge

Total Quality Education for the World's Best Schools

The Comprehensive Planning and Implementation Guide for School Administrators

Series Editor: **Larry E. Frase**

*The authors dedicate this series to the memory of
W. Edwards Deming, 1900-1993*

The Quality Education Challenge

Carolyn J. Downey
Larry E. Frase
Jeffrey J. Peters

CORWIN PRESS, INC.
A Sage Publications Company
Thousand Oaks, California

For information address:

Corwin Press, Inc.
A Sage Publications Company
2455 Teller Road
Thousand Oaks, California 91320

SAGE Publications Ltd.
6 Bonhill Street
London EC2A 4PU
United Kingdom

SAGE Publications India Pvt. Ltd.
M-32 Market
Greater Kailash I
New Delhi 110 048 India

Printed in the United States of America

Library of Congress Cataloging-in-Publication Data

Downey, Carolyn J.
    The quality education challenge / Carolyn J. Downey, Larry E.
Frase, Jefferey J. Peters.
        p.   cm. — (Total quality education for the world's best
schools, v. 1)
    Includes bibliographical references.
    ISBN 0–8039–6129–4 (pbk.: alk. paper)
    1. School management and organization—United States. 2. Total
quality management—United States. I. Frase, Larry E. II. Peters,
Jeffrey J. III. Title. IV. Series.
LB2805.D69 1994
371.2′00973—dc20   94–5964

94 95 96 97 98 10 9 8 7 6 5 4 3 2 1

Corwin Press Production Editor: Marie Louise Penchoen

Contents

Foreword

Lately, *quality* seems to be on the minds of the American public. Every time we turn around, another magazine article, newscaster, or public figure is dealing with issues such as quality control; quality performance standards; world-class, quality schools; or quality time. The Total Quality Management (TQM) movement, has captured the attention of corporate executives, business consultants, members of the health care community, and most recently, practitioners in our public schools.

As applied to schools, the ultimate aim of the quality movement is to help educators transform how they think about their work, how they structure the work environment and make decisions, and how they treat one another. Always quick to embrace the latest concept, a growing number of educators are endeavoring to implement quality principles popularized by the late W. Edwards Deming. Unfortunately, these attempts to transform school systems into world-class, quality learning environments have been somewhat disappointing. Most educators are unfamiliar with the terminology and concepts of TQM, and some believe this is yet another attempt by the business community to tell them how to do their jobs more effectively. They are therefore reluctant and, in many cases, adamantly opposed to accepting any ideas that emanate from the corporate sector.

What is missing for educators is a way to *translate* the ideas about corporate quality so they can be adapted and used in schools. This missing link is precisely what Downey, Frase, and Peters offer in their description and discussion of Total Quality Education (TQE). Using their extensive experience in writing for educational audiences as well as their backgrounds as teachers, administrators, trainers, professors, and consultants, they provide a straightforward, no-nonsense approach. They illustrate how the ideas espoused by quality experts such as Deming, Covey, Juran, and Crosby can be effectively applied to school organizations.

The authors first clarify what quality is and who the customers and suppliers in education are. They then present Downey's Quality Fit Framework, which describes how quality can be infused into school systems. This framework is built on three basic leverage points—purpose, structure, and relationships—that form the basis for applying 18 different premises of quality to school organizations. The translation of these principles into understandable terms and usable strategies is undoubtedly the greatest strength and contribution of the book. Numerous examples, illustrations, and tools provide a wealth of "how-tos" for anyone striving to put the Quality Fit Framework into action. This practical approach "demystifies" some of the language and concepts of TQM, such as constancy of purpose, systems thinking, mobilization of workers, reduction of variation, optimization, and webbed management structure. In addition to outlining specific strategies for each of the 18 principles, the book provides a realistic viewpoint for educators who are considering embarking on the journey towards TQE.

The balanced approach taken by the authors is a key feature of the book. Instead of touting TQE as the panacea for American public education, Downey, Frase, and Peters urge caution in implementing these ideas and acknowledge that it may take several years to fully realize the full effects of quality strategies. Based on their knowledge of educators, school systems, and the change process, they outline potential problems with each of the three leverage points and describe common criticisms leveled at the TQM movement.

Because of this book's practical and sensible approach, educators interested in moving their organizations toward a system in which continuous improvement is the norm can profit from the insights and strategies presented. School board members, superintendents, central office personnel, principals, teachers, and parents can use these guidelines to initiate discussions and to take positive action toward developing a school system dedicated to TQE. Faculty in teacher education and administrator preparation programs will find these ideas stimulating, especially as current and future educational practitioners wrestle with shared governance, customer/client satisfaction, and learning communities. Staff developers who conduct workshops and prepare curricula about quality will discover a host of activities and materials they can use.

Whereas many educators believe their organizations already are committed to TQE, the authors argue that most school systems have not incorporated the 18 premises of the Quality Fit Framework in a systematic, sophisticated way. If TQE is to move beyond speculation and theoretical conjecture, then those educators who take to heart the concepts and practices as outlined here may provide important evidence that quality education *can* exist. This promise alone makes *The Quality Education Challenge* a timely and important contribution to educational practice.

Bruce G. Barnett
University of Northern Colorado

Preface

Will the children we are educating today be able to compete in a world economy? Are we preparing world-class citizens not only for tomorrow but for today? Many educators and business/industry leaders are concerned that the answer is no. Companies are becoming very active in the educational quest for quality to ensure that their workers have the attitudes and capabilities to function effectively in the global economy. We are faced with an international educational challenge that is critical not only to the future of our youth but to our nation.

The quality movement provides an avenue to ensure that our youth will be able to compete in the international arena. Quality is becoming a byword for educators who are attempting to meet this challenge. Just what is quality, and what are its major premises? Can we afford to have quality become just another fad in education—another decade lost—when major educational change is needed? The quality ideals are powerful, and we must pay attention.

In reviewing the literature on the quality movement, we found many similarities and some differences among the major thinkers and gurus of the movement. For many educators, this begins the debate about the definition and major components of quality, identifying our customers, and determining which "guru" to follow. Some educators are becoming entrapped in debates about quality rather than moving toward action. It is time for practitioners to put aside the quality debate and to move forward to implement the many powerful ideas identified by the quality movement.

The educational system needs a major overhaul, and it is our responsibility to become systemic change facilitators in our organizations. Let us focus our energies not on the differences between the major thinkers in the quality movement but instead on the similarities. There is agreement on many significant quality movement beliefs that, if implemented, could provide ample richness of thought for action.

Let us, too, beware of the educator or the entrepreneur who takes something he or she has already been doing and puts the quality label onto his or her strategy, process, or approach. This is often easy to do when the approach seemingly is a useful one. Certainly, for instance, strategic planning is an approach one might use to establish the mission and focus of an organization, but that alone does not make a quality system. Using an outcome-based approach to learning makes sense when thinking about the aim of our organization, but an outcome-based curriculum alone does not mean we have a quality system, nor does a site-based focus. In fact, such approaches are often counter to a systemic approach to management.

We must first have a common understanding of the definition of quality. Then we need to begin to apply the common premises of quality on which the best thinkers in the field agree. There are at least 18 common core premises that can provide a framework, the Quality Fit Framework, which in turn can be used to help us obtain full-fledged quality systems. These premises incorporate many of the ideas of Covey (1989), Crosby (1979), Deming (1982, 1991), Feigenbaum (1991), Glaser (1990), Joiner (1985), Juran (1974), Sashkin and Kiser (1991), and other quality experts.

Chapter 1 begins by addressing the issue of the international educational challenge and serves as a primer for defining quality and various quality premises. For each premise described, several examples of real-life implementation are provided. The main ideas of several quality experts are also briefly examined.

Educators have three leverage points to improve the system: purpose, structure, and relationships. Eighteen quality premises have been categorized under these three leverage points, and this book devotes chapters 2, 3, and 4 to defining each premise and presenting strategies for carrying them out in the school system.

In chapter 2, defining the customer within the mission of the school system is the first step. The mission should be a shared one and, most of all, each person needs to have a sense of mission—a constancy of purpose in all one does. Critical to an organization is the continuous improvement of the processes to achieve the mission. This improvement mode is vital to meeting the ever-changing needs of our customers.

Chapter 3 demonstrates that the second leverage point we have as educational leaders is structure—the way we get our work done. Perhaps one of the most significant ways the quality movement has affected schools is by recognizing that our districts are systems. How can these systems be optimized? Do we now function as rational or irrational systems? Another area examined in the chapter deals with the organizational structure—posing a webbed, integrated structure with cross-functional teams.

The quality movement focuses on process rather than product. This focus is described in connection with how we can influence the inputs and the outputs of our systems. Understanding variation and using quality tools and data are also discussed as part of the second leverage point in chapter 3.

Purpose and structure cannot improve the quality of a system unless dynamic relationships exist among its people (see chapter 4). All participants must work together as a team in an interdependent way. Ensuring that our employees have a shared set of core values and beliefs enhances the constancy of purpose in the organization. How employees are motivated and recognized affects their productivity. Working on faults in the system rather than faults within individuals enhances the likelihood of higher achievements by all. Opportunities to learn and to be a part of a community of learners, as well as communication and feedback, are all part of the relationship leverage point.

Finally, how does one embark on the quality journey? Once a decision to take that first step has been made, chapter 5 presents several suggestions for making significant differences in the lives of our youth.

In chapter 6, the criticisms of Total Quality Management (TQM) in education are examined. To accommodate the talents and the needs of people in the organization and its clients, TQM must be modified.

Carolyn J. Downey
Larry E. Frase
San Diego State University

Jeffrey J. Peters
Kyrene School District

References

Covey, S. R. (1989). *The 7 habits of highly effective people.* New York: Simon & Schuster.

Crosby, P. (1979). *Quality is free.* New York: New American Library.

Deming, W. E. (1982). *Out of the crisis.* Cambridge: Massachusetts Institute of Technology.

Deming, W. E. (1991, March). *A system of profound knowledge.* Participant material distributed at the Quality Seminar, Santa Clara, CA.

Glaser, W. (1990). *The quality school.* New York: Harper & Row.

Joiner, B. (1985). *Total quality leadership vs. management by results.* Madison, WI: Author.

Juran, J. M. (Ed.). (1974). *Quality control handbook* (3rd ed.). New York: McGraw-Hill.

Sashkin, M., & Kiser, K. (1991). *Total quality management.* Seabrook, NY: Duchochon.

About the Authors

Carolyn J. Downey is Associate Professor of Educational Leadership at San Diego State University. She has 22 years of experience in school administration, including 10 years as an assistant superintendent in two school systems and 4 years as superintendent of the Kyrene School District in Tempe, Arizona. She served as an associate in an educational research and development organization for 4 years and left education for 1 year to serve as a health care research consultant. Her expertise includes quality leadership, organizational development, human resource development, curriculum and instruction, and program evaluation. She completed her master's degree in educational psychology at the University of Southern California and her doctorate at Arizona State University. She has published numerous articles, and has written several chapters in books, including *Motivating and Compensating Teachers* (1992), and has authored eight books. She has been an international consultant for over 2 decades, presenting and speaking in hundreds of school systems and for state and national organizations. In 1975, she was recognized as a National Academy for School Executives Distinguished Professor by the American Association of School Administrators.

Larry E. Frase is Professor of Organizational Psychology at San Diego State University. He has 16 years of experience in school administration, including 6 years as assistant superintendent and 8 years as superintendent. He completed his master's degree and his doctorate at Arizona State University. He has published 50 articles in professional journals. *School Management by Wandering Around* (1990) is used in graduate courses and by practicing school administrators. His book *Motivating and Compensating Teachers* (1992) is becoming a hallmark in the educational arena. His most recent book is *Maximizing People Power in Schools* (1992). He has served as a speaker and/or consultant for more than 75 state and national conferences, school districts, and universities. He has received numerous honors and awards at professional conferences and was selected as one of the Top One Hundred School Administrators in the United States in 1985 by the National School Board Association and the American Association of School Administrators.

Jeffrey J. Peters is the Director of Human Resources for the Kyrene School District, Tempe, Arizona. He has had 16 years of success in individual and organizational development in the field of public education. As a teacher of English and reading in New York and Colorado for 8 years, he took a leadership role in instructional and staff development at the junior high school level. His experiences as a grievance representative, negotiation spokesperson, vice president, and president of local education associations affiliated with the American Federation of Teachers and the National Education Association eventually led him to become a UniServ Director with the Colorado Education Association. This position allowed him to hone his skills in negotiations, organizing, labor relations, and systems development. It was during this time period that he became keenly aware of the importance of customer service and the role of stakeholders in decision making. During his tenure as a union organizer and negotiator, he was instrumental in influencing numerous local associations to embrace collaborative bargaining models in lieu of the traditional power bargaining models that had been in use for many years. He is also a trainer and a consultant and has served as a group facilitator in negotiations, conflict resolution, strategic planning, shared decision making, and team building.

✧ 1 ✧

Facing the International Challenge for Quality Education

Many educators and community members believe that today's youths are being adequately prepared to function in a meaningful way in society. Many are beginning to realize, however, that students are not suitably prepared for today or for their future as world citizens. To help our students to function effectively in the 21st century, we will need a major attitudinal change in the way we do our business and many structural changes in our organization.

Meeting the National Challenge for Public Schools

The newspapers, journals, commission reports, and professional literature are replete with criticisms of education in the United States. The criticisms are not new. In the 1950s, Admiral Hyman Rickover concluded that the Soviet Union's launching of Sputnik signaled the failure of U.S. education to maintain our global leadership in science. Popularized books and articles such as "Why Johnny Can't Read But Yoshio Can" (Lynn, 1988) further signaled the alert.

Authors' Note: The effects and the debate regarding Total Quality Management (TQM) are evolving very rapidly. The most current information concerning TQM is carried in the news media and has minimally been addressed in professional books and journals. Hence readers will note the authors' use of daily periodicals such as the *New York Times* and *Education Week* as reference material.

1

The furor over loss of global competitiveness was fueled by the Coleman et al. (1966) study of approximately 650,000 American students. Coleman concluded that neither schools nor the human and material resources in them make a difference in students' academic achievement. The only factors that accounted for variation in test scores were family socioeconomic status and the students' locus of control.

The Coleman study relied on static variables and between-school differences. It was eventually recognized that within-school differences account for much more variation in achievement scores than do between-school differences and that dynamic variables are much more influential than are static variables. Researchers concluded that these design flaws accounted for the results (Cohen, 1983). In a second study, Coleman focused on within-school and dynamic variables and found that schools and their strategies for using resources do indeed account for a great deal of variation in student achievement scores (Coleman, Hoffer, & Kilgore, 1981). Unfortunately, during the 14 years Coleman corrected the design flaws and published the 1981 study, the clamor resulting from the assertion that schools do not make a difference spread widely and ravenously. The year 1983 opened with another attack on education—*A Nation at Risk* (1983). The contents matched and fanned the fright implied by the title. This was followed by 250 additional reports.

All but one, the Sandia Report (Carson, Huelskamp, & Woodall, 1991), decried the failure of the American education system. This report concluded the following: "Serious problems do exist in the American education system. However, there is no system-wide crisis. Much of the current reform agenda is misguided. Progress will only be made by focusing on real, not perceived, problems" (p. 175).

Strangely, this report barely saw the light of day. Some have suggested that it may have been repressed and censored (J. Miller, 1991). Perhaps during the Reagan-Bush years, releasing such a report would have been politically incorrect. Then Secretary of Education William Bennett declared that Chicago schools were "at meltdown," the worst in America ("City's Schools," 1987). The news media and professional educational reports suggest that they still are (Wilkerson, 1993). However, although some school districts such as Washington, DC (American Association of School Administrators, 1991; Horwitz, 1992) and New York public schools (Chira, 1993) are at meltdown or very close to it, others are performing well, as the Sandia reports (Bracey, 1992; Carson et al., 1991; Jaeger, 1992) state.

The skeptical and critical views of American education have reached new heights and strength. This is most dramatically exemplified by the call for choice of schools by parents (Chubb & Moe, 1990) and the experiments in numerous states with private enterprise running schools (Celis, 1993a). The latest effort, Proposition 174, which would have allowed individuals to establish and to operate private schools with public funds, failed in California by a seven to three margin. The number of states entertaining this type of alternative is growing, and the spirit of Proposition 174 is not dead in California. We predict that it will be neatly revised and will appear on the 1995 ballot. Unless the public schools make notable improvements, the next vote will be much closer.

Recent headlines have heralded the success of education in nearly every other industrialized country in comparison to the alleged dismal failure of American education. Some critics of American education consider Japan's educational system the sole reason for Japan's success (Lynn, 1988). Some critics reason that Japan knocked the United States off the top as the world economic power because it built higher quality products at lower prices, and Japan became the global economic leader and received worldwide respect. The United States is searching for a means of regaining its global competitiveness and, of course, education has been targeted as the culprit *and* the hope for the future. Although some critics assert that foreign countries' educational systems have equipped their students with the skills needed in the new economies, the U.S. system has not:

> The overall education level of Americans has increased in terms of schooling and even in fundamental literacy. But demands of the workplace simultaneously have vastly increased. We simply are not keeping pace with the kinds of skills required in today's economy. (Celis, 1993a, p. A1).

Although some Japanese educators see great value in the American educational system, several writers have identified certain aspects of American life as major challenges to the system:

- Large numbers of non- or limited-English-speaking students of monolingual, English-speaking teachers in America (Celis, 1993a)
- Lack of family commitment to education, for example, failure to supervise homework and failure to participate adequately with schools in the educational process (Caplan, Choy, & Whitmore, 1992; Raspberry, 1992)
- Laws and attitudes that require students who continually disrupt class and learning to remain in class (Shanker, 1993b)
- Restrictive policies regarding parental and student accountability (Shanker, 1993a)
- Focus on developing self-esteem rather than learning the basics (Botstein, 1993; Katz, 1993)

Assigning blame for the problems will not help. As Deming has been known to say, "Don't fix blame, fix the system" (Bonstingl, 1992, p. 69). Certainly many systems in American life have contributed to our loss of economic power, and they must be fixed if America is to regain its stature. Schools are not totally to blame for society's problems, including violence, inequity, deteriorating values, poverty, and illiteracy. All Americans, businesses, and social agencies must pitch in.

However, educators cannot afford to use this argument as an excuse or to ignore the problems by claiming they have no control over these external conditions. All sectors of American society must work cooperatively to improve the quality of education and life for American schoolchildren. This cooperation and acceptance of responsibilities by other sectors is beginning (Celis, 1993b).

A recent international study by the Organization for Economic Cooperation and Development, based in Paris, gives hope for redemption (Celis, 1993b). This study found that "American students lag only slightly behind their counterparts around the world in math and science and that a higher than average percentage of American students get college educations." Although these findings are positive, they are insufficient to free education from close scrutiny and pressure for greater productivity.

As Americans, we should tolerate nothing less than "zero" defects, and we must continually strive for improvement. To say that we have no room for improvement or that other societal problems are beyond our control will preclude improvement. As General Motors' success became its enemy, the past success of America's public schools has led to the demise of some, such as the Chicago and Washington, DC school systems. The same can happen to other districts. A shift in thinking about education and school management is needed to stem the tide that is overtaking the public schools.

TQM principles, which have worked well in industries around the globe, offer valuable lessons for education. The best of TQM, combined with sound educational practices, is Total Quality Education (TQE).

Interestingly, Japan gives credit for its success to an American, W. Edwards Deming, and his statistical applications and focus on the worker that evolved into what many now call Total Quality Management. Deming first visited Japan in 1946 as one stop on an around-the-world lecture tour. In 1950, he returned to Japan at the request of Mr. Koyanagi, the founder and director of the Union of Japanese Scientists and Engineers (JUSE), to teach statistical methods. The trip was under the auspices of Douglas MacArthur, the Supreme Commander of the Allied Powers, who was placed in charge of rebuilding Japan's industry (Mann, 1989). Deming is given much credit by both the Japanese and the Americans for bringing the Japanese industry from rubble and a reputation of incompetence to the most effective and highest quality industrial country in the world.

Since Deming began work in Japan in 1950, the Japanese economy has become the envy of other nations (Johnson, 1993). In stark contrast to their reputation for producing cheap and shoddy goods in the 1940s, Japan is now heralded for its high quality products. In a very systematic manner, Japanese industrialists took on corporate giants around the world and emerged as the victor every time. Examples include the American automobile industry; American television, radio, and electronics industries; Xerox; IBM; Harley-Davidson; the Swiss watch industry; and many others. Japan literally stunned the world's corporate giants by winning massive market shares long thought to be sacred holdings of others. They did it by focusing on quality, not profits and market shares. As Deming (1992) asserts, if a high quality product is offered, all else will follow.

Japan, soundly defeated militarily in World War II and reduced to rubble, came back to defeat economically its conquerors, the United States and its allies. Japanese industry accepted Deming and his management philosophies. Soon, other American management and statistical control experts, such as Juran and Feigenbaum, were invited to Japan. Together, these *sensei* (teachers), the determination of the Japanese, and the leadership of Iciro Ishikawa, Japan's top industrialist, transformed their country into an industrial giant respected worldwide as the world's leading exporter of high quality products.

American Resurgence

In keeping with the American spirit, financial, personnel, and technical expertise was given freely to Japan immediately following the war. Japan used it well, and the American economy and pride suffered. Now the gift of TQM has come home and is recognized for its merit. Many American industries have greeted it with cautious but open arms. These industries, with American drive and ingenuity and demands for strong negotiations for fair economic practices, are staging an economic comeback (Sterngold, 1993). True to the American spirit, many American industries are quickly building their reputation for high quality workmanship. General Motors' Saturn and Cadillac Projects, Xerox, Harley-Davidson, Ford, and many others have won back respect, a reputation for quality, and as a result, strong market shares. As Xerox's Paul Allaire, chairman of the board and chief executive officer, said, "We will accomplish our objectives by using leadership through quality" (Allaire, 1993, inside cover). Xerox is back on top. Other American industries once thought to be dead are also regaining respect for quality and reliability. The much-maligned Harley-Davidson motorcycle, the Cadillac STS, the Ford Taurus, GM's Saturn, and yes, the Xerox copiers are selling well all over the world. IBM is staging what it hopes will be a major comeback with its Thinkpad notebook computers. IBM's Bruce Claflin, general manager of Mobile Computing, attributes the success thus far to TQM style management: "It (the Thinkpad) would have been smothered by the old management gridlock, and none of what we have today would have happened" (Lohr, 1993). These successful efforts will have to become continuous to continue the trend toward success.

Confidence in American automobiles has returned to American buyers. Sales in 1993 have exceeded the gains made in 1992. Americans turned to Japanese automobiles in the 1980s because of their quality. Now they are turning to American automobiles for the same reason. President Clinton summed up this trend by declaring that U.S. carmakers are "winning the quality race" (Devon, 1993). This claim may be a bit premature, but the evidence to date is very encouraging.

This is not to imply that TQM is a panacea. It is not. It is only as good as the people using it. This message is captured in a response from Juran when the Japanese requested his permission to name an award after him.

> I did indeed lecture in Japan as reported, and I did bring something new to them—a structured approach to quality. I also did the same thing for many other countries, *yet none of these attained the results achieved by the Japanese. So who performed the miracle?* (Garvin, 1988, p. 184, italics added)

The same could be said of the resurgence of American industry. TQM provided guidelines, but good old American ingenuity, determination, and a sound understanding of theory made it happen. Possibly the best example of this is GM's Saturn Project that, in competition with all cars, is winning numerous quality awards. It is a result of American ingenuity in management, unifying the roles and purposes of management and labor to produce a superior product. Success has not come from protectionist trade agreements; it came from quality. Trade agreements have not yet been resolved between the United States and Japan, although slow progress is being made ("Editorial," 1992). The United States has responded with "quality."

Defining Quality as Applied to Education

Just what is quality? Can it be defined in such a way that we will all agree? Some have said that it cannot be defined, but we believe it can. Quality is an attitude best defined not by us but by those we serve—our customers. Let us look at how others have defined quality:

- *Merriam-Webster's Collegiate Dictionary* (1993) defines quality as *a degree of excellence*—a term applicable to any characteristic.
- Deming (1991) defines quality as *meeting and exceeding the customers' needs and expectations*—and then continuing to improve.
- Feigenbaum (1991) defines quality as what the customer says it is.
- Juran (1974) defines it as *fitness for use*—does it fit the customer?
- The American Society for Quality Control (Johnson & Winchell, 1990) states that quality is *the totality of features and characteristics of a product or service that bear on its ability to satisfy stated or implied needs.*
- Sashkin and Kiser (1991) point out that efforts to meet the needs of customers must be continual because customers' needs and desires change over time.

In this book, we define quality in accordance with Downey's (1992) Quality Fit Framework:

Quality Defined

Meeting, exceeding, and delighting customers' needs and expectations with the recognition that these needs and desires will change over time.

These are the four components of quality:

1. Quality is defined by the customer.
2. Quality is tied to customer needs and expectations (not ours).

3. Quality can have several dimensions of customer satisfaction—meeting, exceeding, delighting.
4. Customers' needs and expectations change over time.

Examining Dimensions of Quality

Helping a group to understand quality can be accomplished by asking each individual to list what quality means to him or her. Then establish small groups, and ask each group to determine the five to seven most frequently mentioned components of quality. Next, merge the groups, and ask them to identify a total of five to seven characteristics of quality. Finally, compare the group list with the dimensions of quality as defined by the American Society for Quality Control (D. Miller, 1993):

Dimension	Definition
Accuracy	Correctness; freedom from mistakes
Aesthetics	How a product or service looks or feels
Assurance	Employees' knowledge and ability to convey trust
Conformance	Degree to which product or service matches established standards (e.g., "right the first time")
Consistency	How closely a product or service resembles those that precede and follow; lack of variation and irregularity
Durability	Useful life of a product or service; how much usage it gives before it deteriorates
Empathy	Caring, individual attention provided to customers/clients
Features	Characteristics of products or services that add to their basic functioning, such as "user-friendly," "induces delight," or "exceeds customers' expectation"
Performance	Primary operating characteristics of product or service such as "on time," or "error-free"

Precision	Degree of refinement with which an operation is performed
Reliability	Dependability of performance over time
Reputation	Image and record of the organization
Responsiveness	Helping customers and providing prompt service
Serviceability	Speed and ease in resolution of problems and complaints
Tangibles	Physical facilities, equipment, appearance of people

Once the lists have been compared, group members can translate these dimensions into the educational arena—using the student as the customer.

Specifying the Customers in Education

Defining quality as possessing characteristics valued by customers leads to a need to identify our customers. This issue is debated often in the halls of education. In fact, a customer is anyone who is being served. Customers are both internal (within the system) and external (outside the system). But our primary customer is the student and our ultimate goal is to ensure that he or she can function in society now and in the future.

Our primary customer (client), then, is the student, who is both an internal and an external customer. While in the system, the student is an internal customer, participating in the learning process. The student becomes an external customer when he or she leaves the school system. At that point, the student becomes the ultimate external customer, functioning effectively in and helping to change society.

Parents not only supply customers but are internal customers themselves, partners in the education of their children. External customers include business, industry, postsecondary training institutions, military institutions, and society in general.

All employees are internal customers of one another. Each is a supplier and a customer to someone else either within or outside of the organization.

One could debate who is the customer of whom. In reality, we are all suppliers and customers of one another. As decisions are made, it is important to recognize the suppliers and the customers in the situation under consideration. Ultimately, however, we must first and foremost be the advocates of the student—not the employee and not the parent—in any decision within a school system. Why? Because the student is our primary and ultimate customer.

Determining Our Product

Defining our *product* is another often-debated topic. The student is not our product; our major product is learning, and we are responsible for spending every moment to add value to each student's capacity to learn. We are a service organization, and the service we provide is the opportunity to learn.

Learning is a two-way interaction; it must involve both the teacher and the students. Students are internal customers in the sense that they bring a unique input to their learning—attitudes, experiences, knowledge, and understandings. Our goal is to interact with them to enhance their capacity to learn. All services in the organization—including both instructional *and* instructional support services—are provided to enhance the learning opportunities for students.

Reviewing the Quality Gurus and the Educational Implications of Their Ideas

There are many "quality" gurus. This book briefly highlights three key players in the quality movement—W. Edwards Deming, Joseph Juran, and Philip B. Crosby.

Identifying Key Points of W. Edwards Deming

Deming, a statistician by profession, is probably the most quoted of all of the quality gurus. In his early years, he worked on product variation in industry. During this time, he developed many theories about how to improve production quality, but his ideas were not immediately accepted in the United States.

In 1950, Deming was asked by a group of Japanese scientists and engineers to discuss with them his beliefs about how to use statistics to control quality. He, along with Juran and a Japanese engineer, Isakawa, is credited with helping the Japanese to turn their business into a world-class economy. Most of Deming's emphasis during this time was on using statistical approaches to reduce variation in production. He also developed concepts of management that have a strong emphasis on employees. These are reflected in his famous "Fourteen Points of Management" (Deming, 1982).

Translating Deming's 14 Points

Deming's (1991) 14 Points	Educational Translation
1. Create constancy of purpose.	Create constancy of purpose toward the mission of the school system.
2. Adopt the philosophy.	Use quality premises to focus the management and leadership of the school system.
3. Cease dependence on mass inspection.	Cease dependence on summative measures of students and staff.
4. Cease doing business on price tag alone.	Develop long-lasting relationships with suppliers and base dependence on lowest cost in resources.
5. Continual improvement of process.	Improve constantly and forever the processes in the school system.
6. Institute training on the job.	Provide staff development opportunities to meet job expectations.
7. Institute leadership.	Leaders must initiate and model paradigm shifts.
8. Drive out fear; build trust.	Remove those structures that create fear in students and staff.

9. Break down barriers between departments.	Work in interdependent ways— break down barriers between groups in schools and between schools and district office.
10. Eliminate slogans, exhortations, and targets.	Eliminate the use of targets, slogans to encourage perform-ance.
11. Eliminate numerical quotas.	Work on the process and do not reward staff based on student achievement gains.
12. Allow pride in workmanship.	Remove barriers that rob staff of pride in their work and stu-dents of the ability to concen-trate on the job of learning.
13. Institute a program of self-improvement.	Have everyone in the school sys-tem help in its ongoing trans-formation.
14. Mobilize all workers to transform the system— do it.	Empower all employees and other stakeholders to trans-form the school system.

Describing Deming's Four Areas of Profound Knowledge

More recently, Deming (1991) developed what he calls four interactive areas of profound knowledge. These are listed below with a brief description.

Area	Description
1. Appreciation of a system	A system is a network or function within an organization that works for the aim of the organization. Management of the system requires knowledge of the interrelationships among all of the com-ponents within the system and of the people who work in it.

2. Knowledge of psychology	People are born with a natural desire to be creative and to acquire knowledge. Intrinsic, not extrinsic, motivators are what bring joy to the workplace. Managers must understand psychology and people.
3. Knowledge of variation	Optimization of the system and improvements in productivity depend on an understanding of variability in processes.
4. Theory of knowledge	Managers must understand the work and make predictions regarding work. Study of these predictions brings new knowledge.

Identifying Key Points of Joseph Juran

Juran is also a quality guru of long standing who worked in Japan for many years. His message is very similar to Deming's. Both feel that top management must lead their organization.

Juran (1974) also lists steps for implementing quality improvements:

1. Build awareness of the need and opportunity for improvement.
2. Set goals for improvement.
3. Organize to reach the goals (establish a quality council, identify problems, select projects, appoint teams, designate facilitator).
4. Provide training.
5. Carry out projects to solve problems.
6. Report progress.
7. Give recognition.
8. Set goals.

Identifying Key Points of Philip B. Crosby

Philip Crosby is a national figure who consults in quality. He is most well-known for his 14 steps (Crosby, 1979) of quality management:

1. Make it clear where management stands on quality.
2. Establish a Quality Improvement Team to run the program.
3. Display nonconformance as a quality measurement.
4. Use cost of quality as a management tool.
5. Raise the level of employees' quality awareness.
6. Provide a systemic way of addressing problems.
7. Prepare to launch a zero-defects program.
8. Define supervisors' training requirements.
9. Conduct a "Zero-Defects Day."
10. Encourage individuals and groups to set goals.
11. Establish an "Error Cause Removal" reporting system.
12. Appreciate and recognize those who participate.
13. Bring together quality champions, and network in quality councils.
14. Do it over again.

Describing the Quality Fit Framework: Purpose, Structure, and Relationships

As a way of synthesizing the ideas of many quality experts, Downey (1992) identified 18 quality premises and designed a model that school systems can use to diagnose their district's specific needs prior to implementing Total Quality Education (TQE). The Quality Fit Framework (Downey, 1992) has been built around three powerful leverage points found in every work setting and identified by Marvin R. Weisbord (1987) in his book *Productive Workplaces*. The three leverage points that can "turn anxiety into energy" are purpose, structure, and relationships. Weisbord (1987, p. 258) states the following:

- Purpose or mission is the business we are in. It "embodies future visions on which security and meaning depend."
- Structure is defined as "who gets to do what" and this "affects self-esteem, dignity, and learning."

- Relationships are defined as the "connections with co-workers that let us feel whole—require cooperation across lines of hierarchy, function, class, race and gender."

The 18 core premises within a framework of the three leverage points are interrelated and must be integrated in a systemic way, as shown in Figure 1.1.

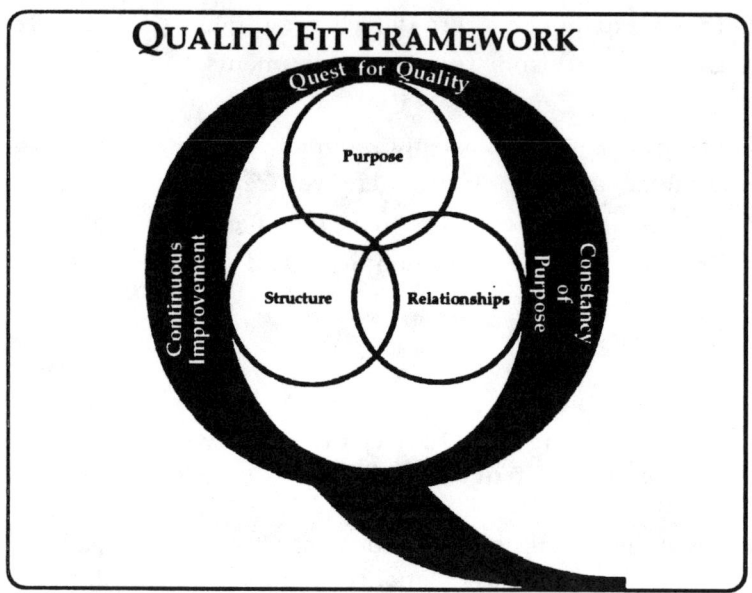

Figure 1.1.

Figure 1.2 summarizes the Quality Fit Framework, and chapters 2, 3, and 4 develop each part of the framework in more detail.

Key Terms and Concepts

Customers. A key ingredient in the definition of quality and a crucial practice in quality management dealing with specifying the actual customers of the organization.

"QUALITY FIT FRAMEWORK"
EIGHTEEN CORE QUALITY PREMISES (DOWNEY, 1992)

Eighteen core premises have been built into a Quality Fit Framework using three leverage points—purpose, structure, and relationships.

PURPOSE: A quality system has four premises related to purpose.

1. Focuses on the customer
2. Provides for a meaningful shared mission
3. Has a sense of mission and constancy of purpose
4. Believes in continuous improvement

STRUCTURE: A quality system has seven premises related to structure.

5. Acts as a systemic organizational structure
6. Focuses on optimization
7. Is a rational organization
8. Has an integrated webbed management structure
9. Focuses on process
10. Understands variation
11. Uses a data orientation

RELATIONSHIPS: A quality system recognizes that organizations are human endeavors and has seven premises related to relationships or dynamics.

12. Mobilizes the workers
13. Has collaboratively, cooperatively interdependent workers
14. Has an organizational culture of shared values and beliefs
15. Understands how people are motivated
16. Recognizes that most failures are attributable to faults in the system
17. Provides for a community of learners
18. Provides for constant communication and feedback

Figure 1.2.

Deming's 14 points of management. Fourteen points provided by Deming for quality management. Each is translated into educational applications in this chapter.

Dimensions of quality. A series of 15 dimensions and respective definitions as defined by the American Society of Quality Control.

Locus of control. A personality variable indicating the extent to which persons view the determinants of their future being due to internal or external factors.

Meltdown. A term coined by Secretary of Education William Bennett to describe the condition of the Chicago public schools.

Profound knowledge. Four areas identified by Deming as profound knowledge requisite to quality management practices.

"Purpose" leverage point. The mission of the organization—embodying future visions on which security and meaning depend.

Quality Fit Framework. Leading ideas of the quality movement gurus organized into three leverage points which can be used by systems to diagnose current implementation of quality.

Quality leverage points. Crucial points that leaders can use to focus energy: purpose, structure, and interrelationships.

Quality premises. Eighteen premises grouped into the three quality leverage point areas. Four are grouped with purpose, seven are grouped with structure, and seven are grouped with interrelationships.

"Relationships" leverage point. The connections with coworkers that give the sense of identity and wholeness. This requires cooperation across lines of formal hierarchy, function, class, race, and gender.

"Structure" leverage point. The organizational structure and distribution of duties among team members. This distribution affects self-esteem, dignity, and learning.

Total Quality Education. A promise to all customers (students, teachers, administrators, and other community members) to continually focus on system improvement and increased productivity through meaningful involvement of all employees in strategic, systemic, and creative leadership and management.

Total Quality Management. An adaptation of Deming's "Quality Management." Definitions of this term vary. These are presented in this chapter.

Union of Japanese Scientists and Engineers (JUSE). A group of Japanese engineers organized by Mr. Koyanagi to bring about the reconstruction in Japan after World War II.

References

Allaire, P. (1993, February 14). *Quality management at Xerox: Address to school district.* Paper presented to San Diego County Superintendents and the San Diego County Education Office, San Diego, CA.

American Association of School Administrators.(1991). *A curriculum audit of the Washington D.C. public schools.* Washington, DC: Author.

Bonstingl, J. (1992). The total quality classroom. *Educational Leadership, 6,* 66-70.

Botstein, L. (1993). The use and misuse of hope. *Education Week, 12*(39), 65.

Bracey, G. (1992). The condition of public education. *Phi Delta Kappan, 74*(2), 104-117.

Caplan, N., Choy, M., & Whitmore, J. (1992, March). Indochinese refugee families and academic achievement. *Scientific American,* 37-42.

Carson, C., Huelskamp, R., & Woodall, T. (1991). *Perspectives on education in America* (3rd draft). Albuquerque, NM: Sandia National Laboratories.

Celis, W., III. (1993a, September 9). Study says half U.S. adults can't read or handle math. *New York Times,* pp. A1, A22.

Celis, W., III. (1993b, December 9). International report card shows U.S. schools work. *New York Times,* p. A1.

Chira, S. (1993, September 5). School opens soon (with luck), to more trouble than usual. *New York Times,* Sec. 4, p. 5.

Chubb, J., & Moe, T. (1990). *Politics, markets, and America's schools.* Washington, DC: Brookings Institution.

City's schools called worst. (1987, November 7). *Chicago Sun Times*, p. 1.

Cohen, M. (1983). Instructional, management and social conditions in effective schools. In A. Odden & D. Webb (Eds.), *School finance and school improvement: Linkages in the 1980's* (pp. 17-50). Washington, DC: National Institute of Education.

Coleman, J. et al. (1966). *Equality of educational opportunity*. Washington, DC: U.S. Government Printing Office.

Coleman, J., Hoffer, T., & Kilgore, S. (1981). *Public and private schools*. Washington, DC: National Center for Education Statistics.

Crosby, P. (1979). *Quality is free*. New York: New American Library.

Deming, W. E. (1982). *Out of the crisis*. Cambridge: MIT Press.

Deming, W. E. (1991, March). *A system of profound knowledge*. Participant material distributed at the Quality Seminar, Santa Clara, CA.

Deming, W. E. (1992, October). *Quality, productivity, and competitive position*. Paper presented at Four Day Quality Seminar, St. Louis, MO.

Devon, L. (1993, May 26). Low interest rates help U.S. vehicle sales. *New York Times*, p. C4.

Downey, C. J. (1992, September). Can the Lone Ranger join the dream team? *Quality Network News*, AASA, Arlington, VA.

Editorial. (1992, February 28). *New York Times*, p. A21.

Feigenbaum, A. V. (1991). *Total quality control* (3rd ed.). New York: McGraw Hill.

Garvin, D. (1988). *Managing quality: The strategic and competitive edge*. New York: Free Press.

Horwitz, S. (1992, February 19). New audit lambastes D.C. school system. *Washington Post*, pp. D1, D5.

Jaeger, R. (1992). Weak measurement serving presumptive policy. *Phi Delta Kappan, 74*(2), 118-128.

Johnson, J. (1993). Total quality management in education. *Oregon School Study Council, 36*, 1-45.

Johnson, R., & Winchell, W. (1990). *Management and quality*. Milwaukee, WI: American Society for Quality Control.

Juran, J. M. (Ed.). (1974). *Quality control handbook* (3rd ed.). New York: McGraw-Hill.

Katz, L. (1993). Reading, writing, and narcissism. *New York Times,* p. A19.

Lohr, S. (1993, June 23). Notebooks may hold key to I.B.M.'s revival. *New York Times,* p. D3.

Lynn, R. (1988). Why Johnny can't read but Yoshio can. *National Review, 15*(21), 40-43.

Mann, N. (1989). *The keys to excellence: The story of the Deming philosophy.* Los Angeles: Prestwick Books.

Merriam-Webster's Collegiate Dictionary. (1993). Springfield, MA: Merriam-Webster.

Miller, D. (1993, August). *Total quality management and the curriculum audit seminar.* Paper presented at the National Academy of School Administrators Workshop, American Association of School Administrators, Gurnee, IL.

Miller, J. (1991, October 9). Report questioning "crisis" in education triggers an uproar. *Education Week,* p. 1.

A nation at risk: The imperative for educational reform. (1983). Washington, DC: U.S. Government Printing Office.

Raspberry, W. (1992, February 21). Despite critics, our schools work. *The San Diego Union Tribune,* p. B6.

Sashkin, M., & Kiser, K. (1991). *Total quality management.* Seabrook, NY: Ducochon.

Shanker, A. (1993a, March 22). Student accountability. *New York Times,* Week in Review, p. 7.

Shanker, A. (1993b, September 5). Fairness—But for whom? *New York Times,* p. E7.

Sterngold, J. (1993). A new old trade policy. *New York Times,* p. C1.

Weisbord, M. R. (1987). *Productive workplaces: Organizing and managing for dignity, meaning, and community.* San Francisco, CA: Jossey-Bass.

Wilkerson, I. (1993, September 8). Chicagoans sigh and adapt as schools are late again. *New York Times,* p. A10.

✧ 2 ✧

Clarifying Purpose and Mission

This chapter examines the leverage point of purpose within the Quality Fit Framework. Four quality premises are addressed: focus on the customer, shared mission and vision, constancy of purpose, and continuous improvement.

Defining the Customer in a K-12 System: Premise One

One of the major changes the quality movement brings to the educational arena is a focus on the customer. In many organizations, employees see themselves as customers of the organization. How can I get more money and work less? Or, how can I get the organization to meet my needs better? The quality focus moves away from employee needs first to customer needs first. It recognizes that the customer is our reason for existence. Our goal is to meet, to exceed, and to delight our customers' needs and expectations.

What is a customer? Customers are those individuals you serve to achieve the purposes of your work. Everyone serves somebody, and everyone is a customer of someone else. The principal's customers, for example, include parents, teachers, and children with whom the principal deals every day. On the other hand, the principal is a customer of the curriculum director and the district superintendent.

Following the quality movement, in effect, turns a traditional table of organization upside down. Instead of the students working for teachers who work for the principal who works for the assistant superintendent who works for the superintendent, it is just the reverse. The superintendent works to serve the assistant superintendents who work to serve the principals who work to serve the teachers who work to serve the students.

Teachers' main customers are the students, followed closely by the parents. Yet the teacher is a customer of the principal.

A customer is the most important person in our work lives. Whether we are speaking to them in person, over the phone, or through the mail, they need our careful attention. Often the customer is perceived as an interruption to our work; however, customers are not an interruption in our work, they are our work. They are doing us a favor by giving us an opportunity to serve and thus, to have a job.

Joiner (1985) indicates that quality leadership begins by giving lasting value to the customer. In the quality movement, we are told to listen to the voice of the customer. In fact, the customer becomes our boss. And the voice of the customer is changing. Figure 2.1 illustrates this change in the primary customer voice:

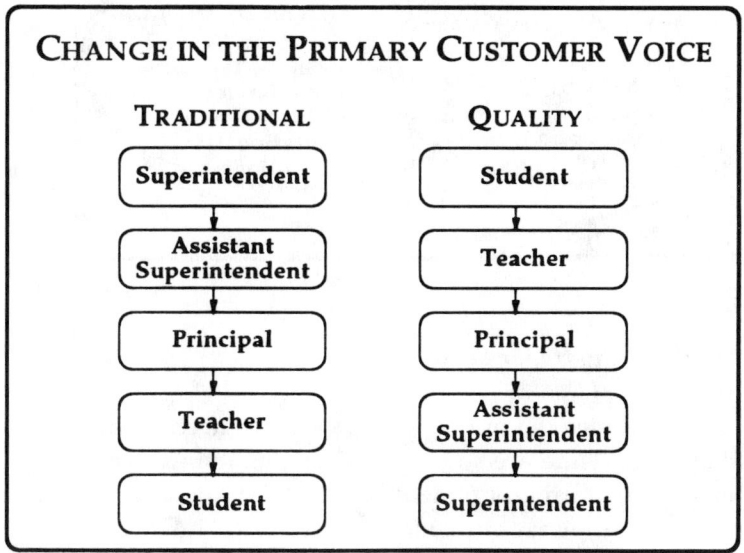

Figure 2.1

Of course, board members are representatives of the community and of the parents, but the quality movement would change their role somewhat. The most important reverse of priority actually deals with the role of students. First and foremost is our responsibility to meet the needs of students now and in the future. Meeting the needs of parents is next most important and so on.

In the school business, we serve many internal and external customers, but our primary customer is the student. Internal customers in the schools include enrolled students, teachers, administrators, other staff, board members, and parents of our students. External customers are students as adults, postsecondary schools, technical schools, business and industry, the military, and society in general. This can be illustrated as shown in Figure 2.2.

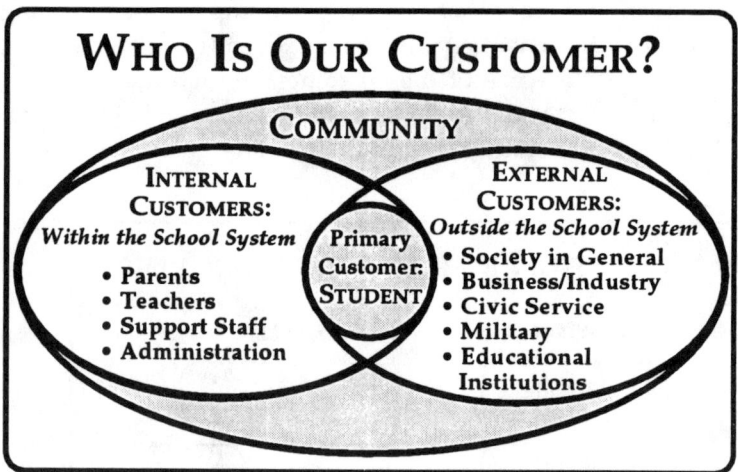

Figure 2.2

Maintaining a Customer Focus

Once we define who our customers are, we need to maintain a customer focus. Here are some ideas for maintaining that focus. First, each of us in the organization needs to know (a) who our customers are, (b) what our customers want, (c) how well we are meeting their needs, and (d) how we are improving the ways we meet those needs.

An activity for employees would be to have them begin to think about being a customer, to describe a recent experience each has had as a customer, and to share that experience by answering the questions in Figure 2.3:

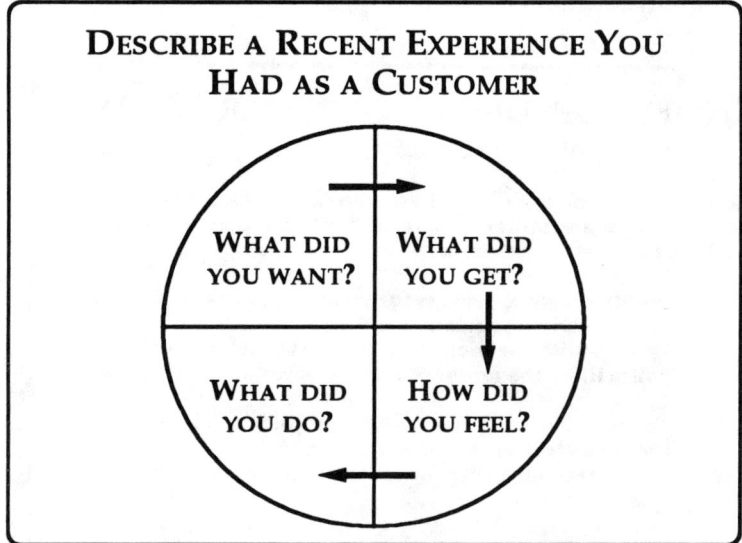

Figure 2.3

Customers who are dissatisfied with a service are more likely to share their feelings with others than those who had a "happy" experience.

Kano (Lillrank & Kano, 1989), a Japanese professor, brings to us the idea of attractive quality. He indicates that quality is defined by expectation and excitement. When one's needs are met beyond an expected level, one adds the attitude of excitement, which has a tremendous multiplier effect. How many of our students are excited about being in our schools? How many experience joy in their learning? And what about our staff, do they find excitement and joy in their work?

Strategies for Defining the Customer

It is highly recommended that the premises of quality in a school system be introduced by having individuals think about who their customers are and how well they are being served. Most customers of staff, other than teachers, are internal customers. Figure 2.4 describes an activity that can be used in training activities to examine customer focus.

UNDERSTANDING CUSTOMER NEEDS
(EXERCISE)

Look around the room and see if you can identify anyone you are a customer of, or a supplier to. Pair up with that person and go through the following exercise.

1. Identify a work process for which someone in this room is your internal customer.
2. Pair up with the identified internal customer. One of you will be the *provider* and the other one will be the *customer*.
3. Together, identify the specific product/service the provider delivers to the customer.
4. Separately, and without consultation, answer these questions:

   Customer: What does it mean to receive this product/ service at the highest quality level? List your needs.

   Provider: What do you think your customer will expect at the highest quality level? List your perception of their needs.

   Both: Rank-order your lists with regard to perceived importance.

5. Compare answers. Does your partner agree with your perception of quality?

Do you realize the value of being able to talk face-to-face with your customer or supplier?

Practice talking face-to-face with your customers in your organization. It is a process that takes only a few minutes, but has a big long-term payoff.

Figure 2.4

There are some key points, therefore, regarding quality and the customer:

- Quality starts with our customers.
- Quality is defined by our customers.
- Customers are the reason we are in business.
- We must know who our customers are.
- Our purpose is to provide lasting value to our customers.
- We should seek out better ways to delight our customers.
- Our customers' needs are ever changing.

The old ways of managing a school system have changed. We are no longer the boss—the customer is. We no longer manage top-down or bottom-up but from the customer in (Belasco, 1993). We involve customers in (a) partnerships, (b) setting goals, (c) giving real-time feedback (now), and (d) allocating resources.

As mentioned earlier, helping staff to understand quality begins with the identification of the individual's customers. In fact, a district could spend 1 year assessing the needs of the customers and changing processes to meet their needs better. Figure 2.5 provides a worksheet to focus staff on customer expectations.

Strategies for Identifying Suppliers and Their Needs

When we look at customers, it is also important to look for our suppliers. Each of us is a customer and a supplier. For students, the teacher is the supplier. And certainly, parents are suppliers to the child as well. The principal is a supplier to the teacher and so on.

In the quality movement, we must not only work to meet our customer needs but we must also help our suppliers to meet our needs. This is rarely done in the school business. For instance, if we are unhappy with a product or service being provided, how often do we work with that supplier to help us meet our needs better? How often have principals talked with upset parents to find that they have not talked with the teacher about their concern? When someone at the district office is not meeting our need, do we go to them and help them understand what we desire, or do we talk about them in the parking lot in an "us-them" mentality?

CUSTOMER EXPECTATIONS WORKSHEET

WHO ARE YOUR CUSTOMERS?

External	Internal
_____	_____
_____	_____
_____	_____
_____	_____
_____	_____

FOR EACH CUSTOMER DETERMINE . . .

Customer _____

What a customer needs _____

How customer needs it _____

When customer needs it _____

Where customer needs it _____

What are the measures of success
in the customer's eyes? _____

Figure 2.5

When suppliers are not meeting our needs, spending time to help them may be very beneficial in the long term.

Figure 2.6. describes an activity that staff can use to determine who are their suppliers and what are their expectations.

An unrelenting focus on our customers is a critical premise of quality. The customer is our driving force and central concern at all times. Providing value in all services to customers is the goal.

SUPPLIERS EXPECTATIONS WORKSHEET

WHO ARE YOUR SUPPLIERS?

External

_____

_____

_____

_____

_____

Internal

_____

_____

_____

_____

FOR EACH SUPPLIER DETERMINE . . .

Supplier _____

What product/service supplied _____

_____

What supplier needs _____

_____

How supplier needs it _____

_____

When supplier needs it _____

_____

Where supplier needs it _____

_____

What are the measures of success in the supplier's eyes? _____

_____

Figure 2.6

Creating a Shared Mission and Vision: Premise Two

All quality experts agree that an organization must have a mission and a vision to provide focus and purpose in the organization. After identifying our customers, a mission statement regarding our intent with those customers creates that focus. A mission statement describes what our service is for. Why are we in the school business, and what does it mean for the student and other customers—internal (e.g., parents) and external (e.g., businesses and industry)? Our mission describes our aim (toward what end) and our general actions (what do we do). Most important, it provides the criteria for making choices. If we do this, we will be furthering our mission. A mission statement is achievement oriented. It is that which we are trying to accomplish for our customers—most important, the students.

Once a mission is established, then a vision is needed to determine how we are going to bring that mission into an ever-evolving reality that recognizes the ever-changing needs of the customer. As stated in Proverbs 29:18, "Where there is no vision, the people perish." Visions look beyond what we are doing today to what we want to be doing in the future. Visions are about imaging the future to create new possibilities.

Obviously, our primary mission involves students. The mission statement seldom changes, although it may be modified occasionally to reflect the changing needs of students. The vision statement, on the other hand, needs to be recreated over and over due to the ever-increasing knowledge of our employees about best practices (benchmarks) and the changing needs of our customers. Nanus (1992) indicates that most leaders realize that visions of the future should not be firmly fixed but should remain flexible to accommodate change.

Describing a Mission Statement

First, the school system needs a mission statement. And all units in the organization need mission statements—the school, the departments—and finally, each individual needs a mission statement. Many organizations have become confused about what a mission statement and a vision statement are and in what order they should be addressed.

Mission is purpose or aim. Lewis Carroll (1988), in *Alice's Adventures in Wonderland*, depicts the need for purpose well:

> "Would you tell me, please, which way I ought to go from here?" asked Alice. "That depends a good deal on where

you want to go," said the cat. "I don't much care where," said Alice. "Then, it doesn't matter which way you go," said the cat (p. 50).

A mission statement for an organization is a broad statement of unique purpose. It has four basic elements:

1. Who are the customers (who receives the service)?
2. Who delivers the service to the customers (who performs the service)?
3. What is the purpose of our service (what ends, what customer needs are being met)?
4. What are the basic means to achieve our purpose (how do we generally achieve that service or product)?

For example, here is a sample mission statement for a school district:

Sample Mission Statement

It shall be the mission of the district to provide experiences that facilitate the growth of students so that they may lead lives, both now and in the future, that are personally satisfying and may contribute to and improve the society that sustains them.

In this statement, (a) the customers are the students; (b) the provider of the service is the district; (c) the purpose is for students to lead lives, both now and in the future, that are personally satisfying and may contribute to and improve the society; and (d) the basic means for meeting that need is providing experiences that facilitate growth.

Here is a mission statement for a superintendent's team:

Sample Mission of the Superintendency

It shall be the mission of the superintendent's team to energize the system's stakeholders toward a shared vision of a desired future to inspire the growth of each employee and enable each individual to fulfill his or her personal, professional, and organizational mission, facilitating individuals and work groups in a way that enhances their capacity to improve the organization continually.

In this statement, (a) the customers are stakeholders; (b) the deliverers of the service are the superintendent's team; (c) the purpose is to bring about a shared vision and continuous improvement in the organization, both through individuals and work groups; and (d) the basic means is through growth of the employees to fulfill personal, professional, and organizational missions.

Each school and department needs a mission statement. Here is one example:

Sample Mission of a Staff Development Department
It shall be the mission of Staff Development to ensure the growth and the development of individuals and groups throughout the organization to improve the quality of student learning. We accomplish this by providing quality learning opportunities using a variety of approaches and resources. We are dedicated to continuous improvement and fostering a learning organization.

Each time a task force or committee meets, it is important for them to have a mission statement linked to the overriding organizational mission. Here is an example:

Sample Mathematics Task Force Mission Statement
It is our mission to provide school district direction in the area of the mathematics curriculum to ensure that students leave our schools with a quantitative sense and competitive mathematics competencies to function effectively in society.

And all individuals in the organization need their individual mission statement. For example:

> **Sample Teacher Mission Statement**
> My mission is to offer instructional leadership that pro-
> vides experiences that facilitate the growth of each student
> to fulfill the district mission.

> **Sample Principal Mission Statement**
> It is my mission to create a community of lifelong learners
> (academically, socially, emotionally, physically) by facilitat-
> ing and ensuring the growth and learning of every commu-
> nity member.

Strategies for Developing Mission Statements

There are many ways to develop mission statements. The following approach (Figure 2.7) could be used to develop a mission
statement.

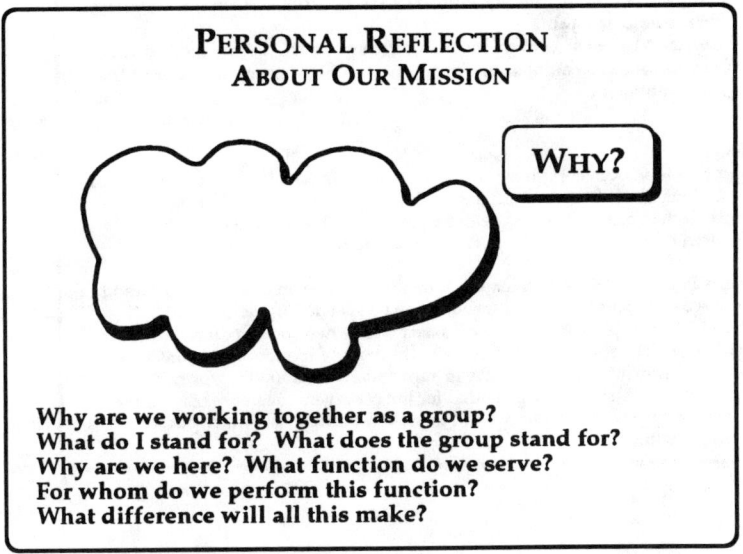

Figure 2.7

Figure 2.8 shows a pyramidal process for reaching consensus on a single mission statement.

THE PYRAMIDAL PROCESS FOR REACHING CONSENSUS

This process is most useful when a group needs to come up with one "answer." It has been used most effectively with developing mission and/or philosophy statements for some specific activity.

1. Thoroughly introduce and discuss the task at hand. For example, if the group is working on a mission statement for the staff development team, the characteristics of a well-written mission should be discussed and agreed to. Everyone needs to have a good grasp of what the final product will look like.
2. Group members are first asked to write their own individual version.
3. After each member has written his/her own draft, pairs are formed. Their task is to reach a consensual agreement on one statement which satisfies them both.
   Note: At this stage it is often necessary to review the "rules" of reaching consensus.
4. Each pair is then joined by another pair, and the consensus-building process begins again.
5. The size of the consensus-building groups continues to grow until one product/statement is arrived at with which every member of the group can agree.

Notes:
This process is seldom completed in a day. Often it is possible to arrive at two or three versions in the first session. It is useful for people to have some time to think about the various versions before trying to reach a consensus on the one and only. Often three or four sessions are necessary to complete the task.

If the group appears to be stalemated — unable to agree on one version or another — the discussion and negotiation process can be speeded up by using a "fishbowl." The opposing groups each select one or two spokespersons for their point of view. The spokespersons come to the front of the room and continue negotiations in front of the rest of the group; thus, a "fishbowl" is formed. An empty chair or two should be provided for the observers to temporarily join the "fishbowl" group whenever they want to make a particular point or put forth a particular argument.

Figure 2.8

For organizations that already have a mission statement, Figure 2.9 indicates a way for the larger community to revisit that statement.

ONE POSSIBLE WAY FOR THE LARGER COMMUNITY TO REVISIT THE DISTRICT MISSION STATEMENT

1. Share the mission statement, how it was created, and other information concerning it to a group at large. Inform the group that their participation in this activity and their work product will be shared with a mission statement ad hoc committee that will consider the input and make changes in the mission statement as necessary.

2. Break the group into smaller groups of 8 - 10. Have them discuss what the mission statement means to them. (10 minutes)

3. Then have members of the group identify the parts of the mission statement that particularly will influence how they serve in their role in the future.

Figure 2.9

Finally, Figure 2.10 provides a strategy for drafting a personal mission statement.

In the school business, our mission needs to be further delineated into student outcomes. The best thinking in the field advocates the use of an outcome-based approach. Such an approach calls for a set of challenging, significant core learnings that all student are to achieve. The outcomes start with broad 12th-grade exit outcomes and move into lower levels' outcomes as illustrated in Figure 2.11.

A sample of proposed outcomes from a school in Wyoming is shown in Figure 2.12.

GOAL

TO DRAFT A PERSONAL MISSION STATEMENT

Materials

1. Copies of the handout "Personal Mission Statement" for each member of the group
2. Blank paper and a pencil for each member.

PROCESS

I.   The facilitator introduces the activity by explaining the goal of the activity and distributes copies of the handouts.
II. Each person in the group silently reads the twenty(20) questions and circles questions they are willing to discuss with a partner. (approximately ten (10) questions.)
III. Partners take turns reflecting on the questions while the other person listens. (Allow 30 minutes for this activity. If additional time is needed, the facilitator will need to adjust accordingly.)
IV. The facilitator asks each person to respond in writing to the questions at the bottom of page 2 of the activity.
V.   Partners share their answers orally.
VI. Each individual writes a personal mission statement using the ideas from above.

Figure 2.10

EXIT OUTCOMES

PROGRAM OUTCOMES

COURSE/LEVEL OUTCOMES

UNIT OUTCOMES

LESSON OUTCOMES

Figure 2.11

TRANSFORMATIONAL EXIT OUTCOMES

PERCEPTIVE THINKERS who develop and use multiple frames of reference to identify, assess, integrate, and apply available information and resources in reasoning, decision making, and complex problem solving.

COLLABORATIVE CONTRIBUTORS who use effective leadership and group skills to foster, develop, and sustain supportive relationships with and between others in culturally diverse work, community, and family settings.

INVOLVED CITIZENS who take the initiative to contribute their time, energies, and talents to improve the welfare of themselves and others and the quality of life in their local and global environments.

INNOVATIVE PRODUCERS who create intellectual, artistic, and practical products that reflect originality, high quality, and the use of advanced technologies.

SELF-DIRECTED ACHIEVERS who formulate positive core values in order to create a vision for their future, set priorities and goals, create options and take responsibility for pursuing these goals, and monitor and evaluate their progress.

ADAPTABLE PROBLEM SOLVERS who anticipate, assess, and resolve the problems and challenges that accompany the rapidly changing political, economic, environmental, and social conditions of modern life.

Figure 2.12

Covey (1992) identifies seven process principles to bring about a mission:

1. Initiate and give constant attention by senior management. Leaders begin the process.

2. Provide for significant early intense involvement by selecting the levels of appropriate management and employees—drafting ideas jointly.

3. Obtain widespread review, feedback, and comments from everyone in the organization.

4. Provide timely communication of the process to all employees and other stakeholders—preview the plan, ask for input, give acknowledgment and appreciation, and report on the final statement.

5. Ensure sufficient time for the process to work—preparation and drafting takes longer than we usually expect.

6. Be committed to follow through concurrent actions by top managers. We need to walk the new talk.

7. Develop subunit mission statements. Each department, faculty member, and work team needs a similar development of its own mission statements.

Describing a Vision Statement

Developing and following a vision creates movement in organizations and in individuals. As mentioned earlier in this chapter, a vision is fluid, ever evolving. It needs to be revisited and recreated on a regular basis. Bennis and Nanus (1985) suggest that a vision of the future is not offered up once and left to fade away. It must be repeated time and again. It needs to become part of the culture of the organization and be reinforced through the strategies used in the organization and through the decision-making process. There are always new circumstances that will change the vision because our world is in constant change.

A vision statement includes the following:

- Where do we want to be in the future?
- What will we look like at that time?
- What will we be doing differently?

A vision is a word picture of the preferred future to which we are committed. It is a dream of how we would like to be. Visions help us to decide what we will spend our time on and, consequently, what we will stop doing or avoid altogether.

A sample district vision statement is shown below.

Sample Vision Statement

We have clarity and commitment to our fundamental purpose of improving the future through enhancing the quality of learning. In addition, all colleagues are dedicated to and passionate about the achievement of the formally adopted mission and embrace the exit student outcomes. The community is an integral part of the goal-setting and decision process of the district and embraces the adopted mission and student outcomes.

We believe in learning that is integrated, meaningful, and implemented in a continuous progress manner where all learners are successful. The learning is designed to accommodate each person's needs, unique gifts, and style of learning while ensuring the common core of student learnings.

Each person is a learner and a teacher. There is great energy and enthusiasm and an environment of collaboration as people come together in small and large groups each day to teach and learn more.

There is an atmosphere of honesty and trust. Each individual assumes personal responsibility for realizing his or her full potential and constantly works toward enhancing the capacity of others to do the same. The community, staff, and students work together and share joint accountability for the outcomes.

We are data driven. We function as a loosely knit interdependent coalition of individuals and groups. Individuals and teams plan, work, and evaluate results with an eye on continually improving learning, products, and the future.

We each realize the value of our individual role and service and also believe we are part of something larger than ourselves. There is a spirit of innovation and cooperation and an acknowledgment of the importance of each individual.

Creating a Shared Vision

Helping others to create a shared vision takes some imagination. Often staff members find it uncomfortable to vision. It requires imagery and moving away from what might seem practical. Often it seems unreal or funny, and guided imagery is often needed. We can, as facilitators, suggest themes and then have the imagery create a corresponding image. Invite others to use their imagination, their creative planning abilities, and to "go for it."

There are many innovative ways to create a meaningful vision for the future. It is strongly suggested that such activities take place in one uninterrupted time block. It is challenging for people to get into the right frame of mind to do this, and it is even harder to get the feeling back if it is lost.

Figures 2.13 through 2.15 present some activities to help bring about visioning.

Hints on Developing Mission and Vision Statements

Barker (1992) indicates that a vision without action is merely a dream. Action without vision just passes time. But vision with action can change the world. How does an administrator maintain the sense of mission and vision? This links to our next section on constancy of purpose as well.

There are many aspects of leadership with respect to mission. First, it must be a shared mission—one developed by the synergy of the group. This is unlike the past thinking that the leader decides the mission and the vision and then influences others to embrace the ideas. Certainly, leaders need a sense of mission and vision, but the difference is that others, too, have an equal sense of mission and vision. When we work together to define the mission and vision, better statements will result. Moreover, we will have a higher probability of meeting the mission and creating the visions. Bennis and Nanus (1985) assert that a vision cannot be established in an organization by edict or by the exercise of mandate.

Fullan (1992) poses the difficult question of whose vision this is. He indicates that the responsibility for vision building is collective, not individual. Collaboration in creating the vision is what is

VISIONING EXERCISE

Idea: Select one of the organization's key values, e.g., "caring."

Encourage participants to image how 5 years from each person would be personally embodying this value day-to-day. What would it look like? What would it feel like?

or

Imagine the year 199_ in our team. What really matters to you? What do you want to create? Imagine it happening. (Play music; guide your colleagues through a mental journey). Encourage group members to draw, paint, sing, dance, etc., images that symbolize their ideas.

Groups of 5-6 people work together. Provide crayons, felt markers, flip charts, overheads, colored pens, tape, scissors, and any other supplies you wish.

The group decides whether or how to make use of the material.

After 90 minutes, each group sends 2 members to visit 2 other groups. This "visit each other" intervention is a way of bringing new perspectives and energy into the discussions.

Sharing visions in songs, poems, limericks, sketches, collages, models, and drawings.

These descriptions will capture the values of group members and the beginnings of innovations.

At the next session, revisit the essence of each and begin to capture themes.

Figure 2.13

important, not complying with the superintendent's or the principal's vision. All stakeholders should be involved. Patience will be needed because many voices may initially create conflict, but through a collaboration process, conflicts will be resolved.

The task of synthesizing an appropriate direction for the organization is complicated by the many dimensions of vision that may be required. Six leadership requirements (source unknown) should be considered:

VISION SCENARIOS –
5 TO 10 YEARS FROM NOW

Peter Block tells us that a vision is lofty. It captures the imagination and the spirit. It comes from the heart. It is unique and compelling.

He offers these guidelines:

1. Don't focus on being number one. Concentrate on the contribution your school or group will make instead.

2. Don't be too practical. A vision of greatness is spiritual and idealistic. It should be realistic yet ambitious.

3. Focus on the children and other clients. This is the key for long-term survival.

4. Consider how you treat each other as well.

5. If your vision sounds like motherhood and apple pie and is somewhat embarrassing, you are on the right track.

6. Be patient. Developing a powerful vision takes time and effort. Give it time to grow and develop.

Figure 2.14

- *Foresight,* so we can determine how the vision fits into the way the environment of the school system may evolve
- *Hindsight,* so that the vision does not violate the traditions and the culture of the school district
- A *worldview* within which to interpret the impact of possible new developments and trends

---

VISION EXERCISE

Imagine that it is five years in the future. You are staff members of _____ school. It is a well-known center of learning. Its reputation is so positive that people from other parts of the province have read about it. Some people have moved to this district specifically so that their children may attend this school.

A feature article is to be written describing this wonderful school. Will you take a few moments now to write down your vision of this nearly perfect place? Write in journalistic style:

• What happens here that makes it such a special place?
• What elements would a visitor notice in the classrooms, hallways, and even outside the building?

You may include physical things, but be sure also to think about behaviors. How do people act here? Teachers with other teachers? Teachers with students? Students with one another? Are parents involved?

Why do the students like it here? Why do teachers like it? Parents? Administrators?

What was your role in bringing this about?

Figure 2.15

• *Depth perception,* so that vision can be seen in appropriate detail and perspective
• *Peripheral vision,* so that the possible responses of stakeholders to a new direction can be comprehended
• *Revision,* so that all visions previously synthesized are constantly reviewed as the environment changes

Figure 2.16 provides a road map for the development of mission and vision statements in an organization.

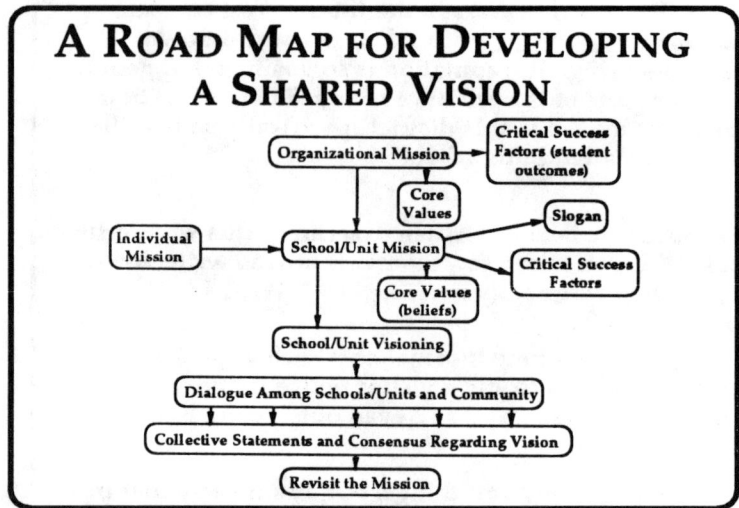

Figure 2.16

In discussing shared visions, Senge (1990) indicates that each person's personal vision must be translated into shared visions. It is important to bind people together around a common identity and sense of destiny.

Providing for Constancy of Purpose: Premise Three

One of Deming's (1982) 14 points is to create constancy of purpose toward improvement of products and services. The focus is on the purpose or aim or mission rather than the results. Many school districts have a mission statement, but is that mission alive and well in the system? Is it used to focus the energies of staff members? It is interesting to ask staff members in school districts that have mission statements about the essence of the mission statement. Often staff members have no idea.

Downey (1993) writes about breathing life into the mission. She states that writing a mission statement is the easy part. Creating a continuing sense of mission in the organization becomes the challenge. We should daily ensure, first, that we personally have constancy of purpose. Second, we need to provide an environment in which all employees have a missionary zeal toward the mission of the organization.

Having a sense of mission or constancy of purpose means that each of us has a passion about the aim of the organization and a commitment to ensuring that decisions, actions, and thoughts are aligned with the mission of the organization. Constancy of purpose creates a unity of spirit and an opportunity for continuous improvement. It creates a sense of role efficacy for each staff member. Each of us should be able to describe how the activity we are currently engaged in makes a difference toward the mission of the system.

Often when mission statements are first developed there is energy around that mission. Over time, however, if we are not diligent and focused in our own desire for constancy of purpose, the mission statement can become just another plaque on the wall. There are many competing priorities of stakeholders in school systems that can move an organization away from the mission, for example, employee interest or special interest groups. All too often our commitment to our ultimate customer—the student—waivers.

Downey (1993) suggests several strategies for maintaining a constancy of purpose toward the mission:

- Ask in every situation whether this action, activity, thought, or behavior contributes in some way to adding value to our students and their learning.
- Have staff members and other stakeholders answer the question for each decision point of how the decision facilitates the fulfilling of the mission.
- Search out opportunities in all discussions to coach and influence others to think about and act on the mission.
- Revisit the mission and vision statements regularly to revitalize employee commitment, and have individuals check their work groups and their own activities for alignment with the mission.

- Have all work groups prepare and review mission statements in alignment with the system mission—groups such as cabinets, administrative teams, school faculties, department staff, grade-level groups, and interdisciplinary teams.
- Have groups identify critical success factors that will create opportunities to bring about the mission and vision.
- Provide mission and vision orientation for new employees, and have them prepare their own mission and vision statements.
- Place mission statements in documents such as yearly targets, annual reports, newsletters, letterheads, and name cards.
- Critique agendas for meetings (board permanent teams, faculty meetings, ad hoc work groups) for value to the mission. Debrief meetings and ask whether the discussion and the proposed actions helped us to reach our mission and vision.
- Ensure that governing board meetings start with a focus on learning and that the student performance activities of work groups are tied to the mission and vision.
- Establish yearly district process goals and strategies tied to the mission and vision.

Of all the strategies, however, the most important is how we, as educational leaders, personally commit ourselves to the mission and vision. If we believe, we will influence others through our own behavior. Establishing mission and vision statements is dynamic and synergistic, but once born these statements must be constantly nourished.

Maintaining Continuous Improvement: Premise Four

The last quality premise in the purpose leverage point of the Quality Fit Framework is the powerful idea of continuous improvement. Many educators are beginning to use the term *Continuous Quality Improvement* (CQI) rather than Total Quality Management (TQM).

Deming's (1982) fifth of his famous fourteen points is to improve constantly and forever the system. There are two very important words in his point—*constantly* and *forever*. It has been said that quality is a never-ending journey.

We need to be obsessed with the quest for quality (Joiner, 1985), something we relentlessly pursue. Continuous improvement occurs when we purposively and systematically plan organization change and individual change as we seek out ways to improve quality in our school systems.

Student needs are ever changing, and thus our service to them must continually change. As society changes, so must we change the services we provide so that students can function in that society. Certainly, from this perspective, we need to improve. But even if this need did not exist, we would need to improve our districts continuously.

Continuous improvement begins with each one of us committing to change. We must be the change we want to see in the world (Ghandi, 1984). It requires a commitment to continuous learning. Many quality experts say, "If we keep doing what we've been doing, we will keep getting what we've been getting."

Understanding Paradigms, Kaizen, and Hoshin

Continuous improvement means that we need to change our mental models constantly (Senge, 1990). Mental models or paradigms are the way we set rules or regulations that define our thinking. Joel Barker (1992) identifies six main points about paradigms:

1. Paradigms are common.
2. Paradigms are useful.
3. Sometimes our paradigm becomes the new paradigm.
4. People who see outside the paradigms often operate on the fringe of the organization.
5. People who are practitioners of the old paradigm but choose to change have to be courageous.
6. We can choose to change our paradigms.

Some of the paradigm shifts that quality brings to school districts are listed in Figure 2.17. A good activity is to have employees note differences between the old and the new paradigms and then to assess our own school district in terms of where we are with respect to the paradigms.

CQI PARADIGM SHIFT

OLD PARADIGM	NEW PARADIGM
Technology/machine resources	People as valuable resources
Narrow tasks, simple tasks	Broad tasks, multiple skills
External control: mandated procedures	Self-control: teams and departments
Hierarchical, autocratic style	Flat organization, participative style
Competitive	Cooperative
Alienation: "It's only a job"	Commitment: "It's *my* job!"
Low risk taking	Challenge, creativity, and high risk taking
Maintain the status quo – don't rock the boat	Continual improvement and innovation
Avoid or resist change	Stay on top of change

What general difference do you see between the old paradigms list and the new paradigms list?

Figure 2.17

The Japanese word for continuous improvement is *kaizen*—to produce consistently better products and/or services by striving for improvement day by day. We need to search for ways to function better in our work processes and to make small daily improvements. This requires risk taking and constant persistent experimentation. Staff members will need to see change as a friend rather than something to fear.

Another Japanese word used in continuous improvement thinking is *hoshin*. Hoshin is very much like program evaluation and review technique (PERT) charts or strategic action plans. It is a fact-driven, structured process that focuses on improvement opportunities and key system problems. It is a set of plans to develop capability and to bring about breakthrough objectives. It includes a set of action plans for all parts of the system.

Using the PDSA Cycle

Continuous improvement requires rigorous use of facts and analysis. Deming (1991) supports the Plan-Do-Study-Act (PDSA) cycle.

> *Plan.* To plan we must have knowledge of the process to be improved. How is it functioning now? Is it stable? Determining what to change and how to change the process requires prediction and data on common causes. If-then predictions need to be made about the results of a planned course of action.
>
> *Do.* Test the planned change on a small scale.
>
> *Study.* Study the results of the change and check the prediction. Determine whether there is evidence of process improvement.
>
> *Act.* Take action based on the results of the study. If the process is stable at an improved level of performance, institutionalize this change throughout the school system. If the study shows no evidence of improvement, abandon the change.
>
> *Continue the cycle.*

Deming (1991) attributes the problem-solving cycle to Shewhart. Senge (1992) indicates that when he studied the Deming and Shewhart cycles he could trace them to John Dewey's studies in education. The PDSA cycle is, in essence, a problem-solving set of strategies. Sashkin and Kiser (1991), in talking about the PDSA cycle, indicate that it may seem simple, but it must be based on rational thinking and problem solving.

Using "Best Practices" for Benchmarking in School Systems

Perhaps one of the most useful quality ideas in continuous progress is benchmarking. Benchmarking originated with land surveys where a mark on a permanent elevation was made to serve as a reference point. Eventually, it became a standard by which things are measured. The rise to benchmarking traces to the 1970s and Xerox's replacement of *its* best with *the* best.

Benchmarking is now defined as the practice of searching for new methods, practices, and processes that are not limited to your own organization. It is the consistent researching for new ideas and implementing them to obtain the "best of the best." The idea is to first study your own school district to find the best practice and to set that as a benchmark for the entire district. Strategies for bringing about that change need to be instituted in order for that practice to be widespread throughout the district. When this is accomplished, it is called "standardization" in the quality movement. Standardization is the implementation of the best known way for doing our work. It reduces variation and maintains previous improvements.

While we are standardizing a best practice districtwide, we need to be searching for the next best practice in the process under consideration. Here, we examine other school districts known as "best" in the implementation of a practice and bring their strategies to our district. Next, we would investigate other educational entities and others involved in similar processes regardless of the business.

Eventually, we would become the best in the field. This is called "world-class." World-class is a distinction given to those organizations, regardless of their business, that perform a function or a process better than any other organization.

School districts that work on incorporating "best practices" into the district have much to do. The restructuring movement has brought about many ideas in governance, shared decision making, curriculum design, instructional strategies, assessment approaches, grouping and staffing processes, personnel approaches and budgeting. The wealth of research and best practices available to improve our schools make it an exciting and challenging time to be an educator.

We must not wait for problems before we improve. The chart in Figure 2.18 illustrates the traditional approach to improvement efforts. What we need to work toward are incremental improvement efforts, which are illustrated in Figure 2.19.

Not only must we work for continuous improvements but breakthroughs. Continuous improvement efforts are a series of

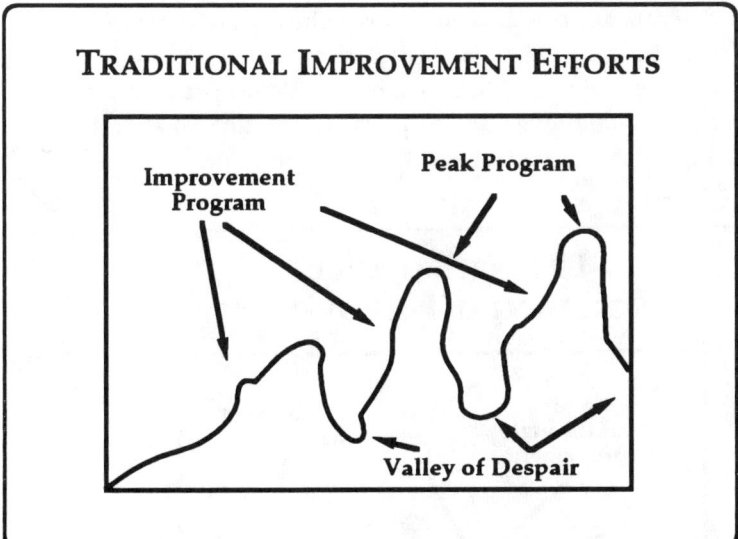

Figure 2.18

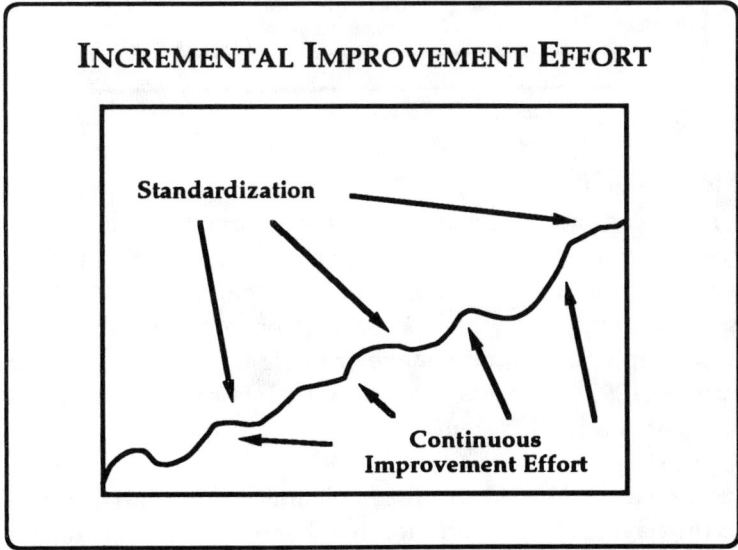

Figure 2.19

small, discrete improvements over a short time interval that require little time or financial investments. Breakthroughs, on the other hand, require major shifts in quality improvements. They take longer to achieve and require significant financial investments. Figure 2.20 illustrates breakthrough efforts.

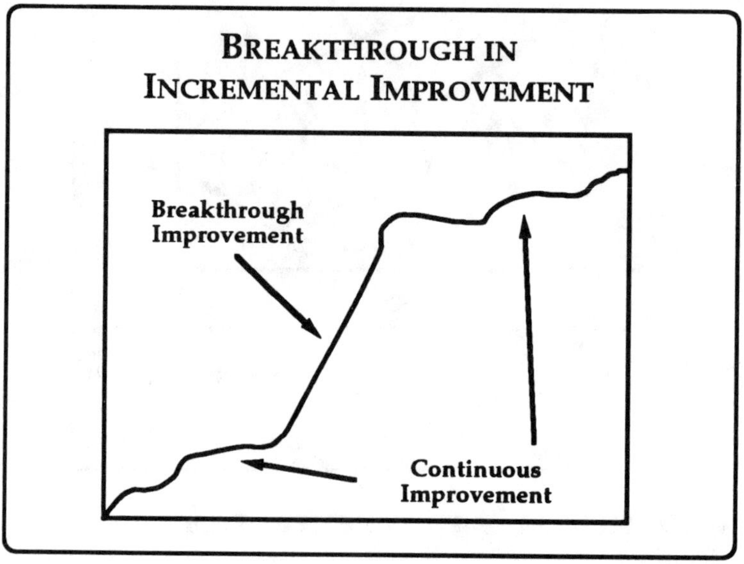

Figure 2.20

As leaders in education, we must provide time for people to study any recommended changes. Have groups think about the last time they made a suggestion about changing the way in which things were done and the suggestions posed. Then have them discuss what happened with that suggestion. Was the school system leadership open to that change or not?

Neuroth (1992) suggests the following strategies for addressing change in a school system:

- Set goals grounded in process changes—do not start until you have defined and stabilized the system. Setting improvement goals in the absence of knowledge about processes is a useless exercise.

- Unite the entire school system in the improvement process. Individuals can make some progress, but teams are the most effective change agents.
- Use a disciplined method of inquiry, for example, the PDSA cycle.

Summary

This chapter presented several key quality premises tied to the system leverage point of purpose. The leverage point works in an integrated way with the other two leverage points—structure and interpersonal relationships. A customer focus and a mission are first steps in moving toward continuous improvement.

Key Terms and Concepts

Benchmarking. The practice of searching for new ideas and implementing them to obtain the "best of the best practices."

Best practices. Those practices considered to be state-of-the-art or "world-class." Best practices are used in benchmarking.

Constancy of purpose. One of Deming's 14 points—to create a focus on the purpose, aim, or mission rather than results.

Continuous improvement. Constantly working to improve the system to better meet the customer's needs.

Customer. Those individuals served by the purpose of an organization's or individual's work.

Hoshin. A fact-driven, structured process that focuses on opportunities to improve.

Kaizen. Day-to-day continuous improvement to produce better products and/or services.

Mission statement. Broad statement of unique purpose that includes four elements: Who receives the service (customers), who delivers the service, what is the purpose of the service, and what are the means to achieve the purpose?

Paradigm. The way we set rules and regulations that define our thinking.

PDSA cycle. A problem-solving cycle developed by Shewhart that includes four steps based on rational thinking and problem solving: plan, do, study, and act.

Suppliers. The people who supply service to the customer, for example, for students, the teacher and the principal are suppliers and the principal is a supplier to the teacher. Each person becomes both a supplier and a customer.

References

Barker J. (1992). *Paradigm pioneers* (Videotape). Burnsville, MN: Chart House International.

Belasco, J. (1993, July). *Total quality management seminar.* Paper presented at the meeting of 21st Century Education, San Diego State University, CA.

Bennis, W., & Nanus, B. O. (1985). *Leaders: The strategies for taking charge.* New York: Harper and Row.

Carroll, L. (1988). *Alice's adventures in wonderland* [A Tom Dorharty Book]. New York.

Covey, S. R. (1992, November). *The mission statement process.* Handout at the Goal/QPC Convention, Boston, MA.

Deming, W. E. (1982). *Out of the crisis.* Cambridge: MIT Press.

Deming, W. E. (1991, March). *A system of profound knowledge.* Participant material distributed at the Quality Seminar, Santa Clara, CA.

Downey, C. (1993, Spring). Breathing life into the mission. *Quality Network News,* p. 2.

Fullan, M. (1992). Visions that blind. *Educational Leadership, 49*(5), 19-22.

Ghandi, M. (1984). *Collected works.* Delhi, India: Ministry and Broadcasting.

Joiner, B. (1985). *Total quality leadership vs. management by results*. Madison, WI: Author.

Lillrank, P. & Kano, N. (1989). *Continuous improvement: Quality circles in Japanese industry*. Ann Arbor: University of Michigan Press.

Nanus, B. (1992). *Visionary leadership*. San Francisco: Jossey-Bass.

Neuroth, J. (1992). *Total quality management handbook*. Lansing, MI: On Purpose Associates.

Sashkin, M., & Kiser, K. (1991). *Total quality management*. Seabrook, NY: Ducochon.

Senge, P. M. (1990). *The fifth discipline*. New York: Doubleday.

Senge, P. M. (1992, November). *Quality and Management*. Paper presented at the National Goal/QPC Convention, Boston, MA.

✧ 3 ✧

Understanding Structure Through Systems Thinking

This chapter presents seven quality premises that are linked within the Quality Fit Framework to the leverage point of structure. Premises presented are appreciation of a system; optimization; rational organization; integrated, webbed structure; process focus; variation; and data orientation.

Defining Systems Thinking in a School District: Premise Five

One of the most powerful ideas the quality movement brings to our school systems is the concept of systems thinking. *Merriam-Webster's Collegiate Dictionary* (1993) describes systems as regularly interacting or interdependent groups of items forming a unified whole. To Deming (1991), a system is a network of functions or activities within an organization that works together for the aim of the organization. Therefore, the aim of the school system must be clear to everyone in the district.

Leaders in school districts are responsible for orchestrating the district as a system. Management of school districts, therefore, requires knowledge of the interrelationships among all components within the district and of the people who work in it.

Senge (1990) has been a major influence in this area. His fifth discipline is systems thinking. He defines systems as *groups of interdependent components, people, and processes with a common purpose.* Systems approaches require changes in thinking from

- Straight line to circular causality
- Independent to interdependent relationships
- External to internal focus
- Knee-jerk, short-term, fragmented problem solving to proactive, long-term, holistic solution seeking
- Thinking something is wrong with a person to acknowledging a problem in the system

Two configurations illustrate the concepts of systems thinking versus a fragmented system. Figure 3.1 is an example of a fragmented system. A systemic school system is illustrated in Figure 3.2.

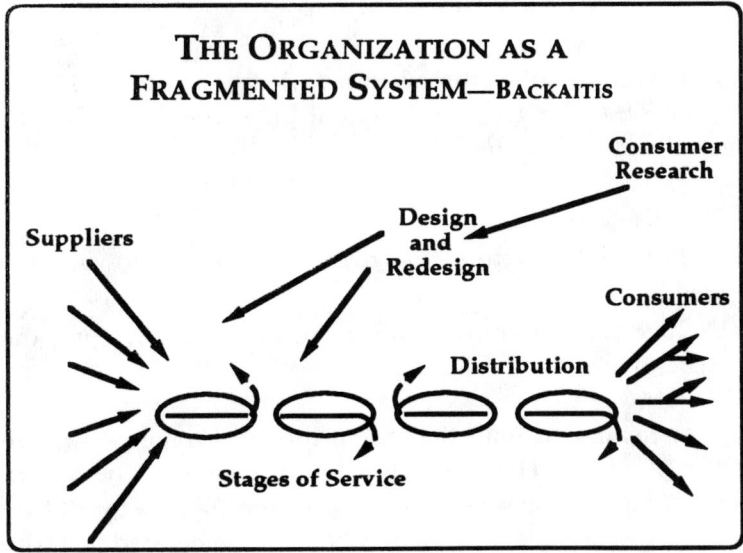

Figure 3.1

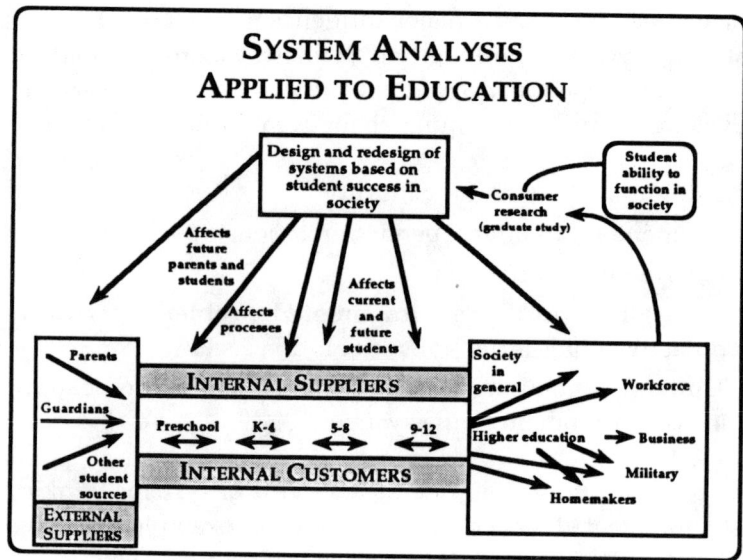

Figure 3.2

Senge (1990) identifies three leverage decision points within a system that offer the greatest potential for correcting problems permanently. These are the following:

- Identify the goal.
- Identify the structure that drives the system toward the goal.
- Deduce the dynamics that will result from changing the structure.

It is interesting to note that these three leverage points are similar to Downey's (1992) Quality Fit Framework. The key to systems thinking in the school business is to recognize the nature of relationships, deduce the dynamic behavior generated by those relationships, determine the high leverage points of change, and then act on those leverage points.

Senge (1990) points out several important ideas regarding systems thinking:

- The world is interdependent and dynamic with multiple events happening simultaneously.
- The focus of systems thinking is on patterns of events and the structures generating behavior.
- The most important effects are often delayed.
- The emphasis needs to be on internal locus of control of people and leadership in terms of influence.
- In solving problems, there are no final right answers, but there are better answers.

Another important concept Senge (1990) brings to our thinking about school systems is the idea of mental models—the way we think about things. All of us build mental models (paradigms) and simulate them all the time. Systems thinking is a skill developed to change the degree to which we can deduce the dynamic behavior of our mental models. Visioning helps us to change our mental models. Paradigm shifts in the school business come from constantly keeping ourselves open to new ways of thinking and to changing mental models.

Systems thinking is needed more than ever today because we are becoming overwhelmed by the complexity of our society. We now have the capacity to create far more information than anyone can absorb, to foster far greater interdependency than anyone can manage, and to accelerate change beyond anyone's ability to keep pace (Senge, 1990). It is important that we provide the schools the capability to pull together the diverse functions and talents of employees to form a productive whole.

Understanding Several School System Disabilities

Senge (1990) identifies several disabilities within organizations such as our school districts. One of them is the notion that the enemy is out there. Systems thinking shows us that there is no outside. We and the cause of our problems are part of a single school system. Systemic structures influence behavior over time. These interrelationships are among key organizational variables, not between people.

One of Deming's (1982) points is to break down barriers between departments and staff. Competition among departments, divisions, and schools only encourages further fragmentation. Even when a school district shares the same goals, we often find competition among various schools and divisions.

Another important ingredient in understanding systems thinking is recognizing that most of us tend to use decision-making processes that provide short-term fixes rather than long-term effects. Two of Senge's (1990) learning disabilities help us to understand this. First, he says that we often have a fixation on events. This leads to "event" explanations. Longer patterns of change lie behind the events, and such a focus keeps us from understanding the causes of those patterns.

The second learning disability Senge (1990) calls the "Parable of the Boiled Frog." The parable is about a frog that jumps into a pot of water on a stove. Gradually, the fire is turned up, and the frog continues to adjust to the temperature until it dies. Senge indicates that we are geared for sudden changes in the school business, not slow, gradual changes. Gradual process change often poses the greatest threat to our school system. He states that today's problems are a consequence of yesterday's solutions. Long-term effects result from systemic problem solving.

Often our solutions merely shift problems from one part of a system to another, with the new problem often going undetected for a while. Short-term solutions work for the short term—these are low-leverage interventions. They often lead to long-term dependency. Such decisions, Senge (1990) says, can leave the system fundamentally weaker than before. In the school business, we must work for high-leverage interventions for long-term effects. The easy way out usually leads in. He indicates that cause and effect are not closely related in time and space. The areas of highest leverage are often the least obvious.

Areas focusing on mission and vision for schools and school districts are major leverage points and often provide breakthrough processes. Certainly, moving toward team approaches that use a collaborative decision-making process is a strong leverage point. Focusing on the interpersonal relationships that provide strong dynamics brings about an environment for change.

Implementing Systems Thinking in Schools

Systems thinking enables school district leaders to turn complex data, disparate facts and figures, and mixed messages of all kinds received from both within and outside the school district into an overall organizational strategy that has a clear and consistent shared vision based on the personal mastery of each member (Senge, 1990).

There are many strategies we can use to bring systems thinking into our schools. Certainly, team decision making, especially when the team is composed of cross-functional employees and other stakeholders, is a major approach. It is also time for us to begin to realize that we cannot treat any idea in the system in a "keep it simple" mentality. This will lead only to short-term fixes.

Providing for an Optimized School District: Premise Six

A second quality premise of the structure leverage point is that of optimization. It links closely to the concept of systems thinking. Deming (1991) indicates that to obtain quality the system must be optimized. And during such a process, not all departments and/or divisions in a school system can be optimized. He believes that it is the obligation of a department or other unit in the school system to contribute its best to the system, not to maximize it own production or service. Some components of a school system may need to operate at a loss to optimize the entire system. Optimization for everyone should be the basis for negotiation between any two people, divisions, or groups in the school system.

There are many examples of how optimization and suboptimization can work in a school system. One school system worked on providing more time for learning. Classroom time was to be optimized to the suboptimization of other things. This led to many changes, such as

- Shortening the time between class periods
- Making announcements over the intercom only during the first 5 minutes and the last 5 minutes of the day

- Computerizing attendance by connecting classroom computers to a mainframe
- Leaving items that were left at home by students and delivered by parents at the office for children to pick up rather than having parents take them to the classroom
- Considering effective teaching practices (e.g., how to increase engaged rates, transition time)
- Having parents schedule routine dental and medical appointments after school
- Ensuring fund-raising activities never interfered with instructional time
- Providing elementary strings and band before- and after-school activities rather than holding them during the day
- Timing of all pull-out programs so that students attending such programs were taking instruction in the same discipline—a type of regrouping

An instructional example of optimization occurred when a school system determined that it would provide flexibility of instructional resources to optimize the teacher's instruction over the suboptimization of budget considerations for the bulk purchase of materials.

Yet another example is illustrated by the poor optimization of transportation schedules. The school day was structured in such a way that those children who rode buses to school actually had 20 minutes less instruction daily because the bus arrived 5 to 7 minutes after the school day had begun and left 13 to 15 minutes before the school day ended. Twenty minutes a day for 180 days came to 60 lost instructional hours or almost 2 weeks a year.

Once employees understand that not every unit can be optimized, they will identify numerous areas where we can begin to work. They key is to determine what we wish to optimize.

Being a Rational Organization: Premise Seven

Many individuals who have studied school districts consider them to be irrational organizations. A rational organization is one in which the activities of the school district are related to its goals and one that is able to relate internal activities to its purposes (English, 1987).

One of the problems we have as educators is that we often encounter resistance in trying to attain a political consensus about precise schooling outcomes. School goals often remain nebulous, not because we do not know how to write them in a precise way but because those groups that control schools desire ambiguity as a matter of continuing to control them (English, 1987).

Scholtes (1988) asserts that work is not haphazard. It can and must be studied, analyzed, and scientifically dissected. Deming (1991), in his theory of knowledge, indicates that for an organization to be rational, prediction, observation, and theory are required. He describes administrators' responsibilities as looking ahead, predicting, and changing the organization. According to Deming, rational planning requires predicting certain conditions and behaviors and comparing performance. These are powerful ideas that can improve our school systems.

Fenwick English (personal communication, November 1-2, 1992) contends that a rational organization develops goals and translates them into activities that are congruent with the goals. It then appropriates resources based on goal priorities, and translates both into tangible jobs to be performed and subsequently evaluated. Feedback is obtained from evaluation, and the cycle is repeated until the desired results are obtained at the lowest possible cost. He further states that school systems are often reactive rather than proactive: we act first and then invent reasons for our actions.

English (1988) identifies a critical rationality that needs to be addressed in all school systems—and that is the degree of alignment of the written, taught, and tested curricula. Quality control is movement toward the unity of these three elements. A rational system has the capacity to determine the expected curriculum through the written curriculum, to move the delivery of curriculum to be aligned with the written curriculum, and to design and implement testing programs aligned with the written curriculum. This is illustrated in Figure 3.3.

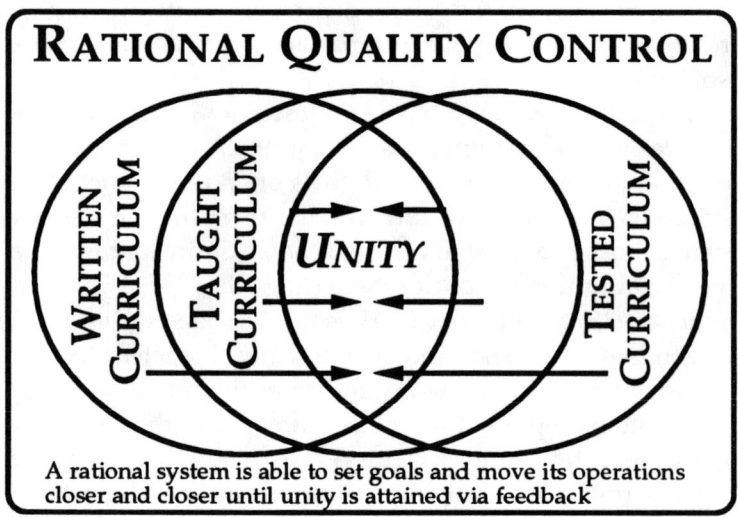

Figure 3.3

A rational school system establishes long-range plans for movement toward the system's mission and vision. Such plans will have the following minimal components:

1. *Mission.* General purpose, beliefs, and educational goals of a school organization. The mission is the foundation on which all educational programs and services are built. It describes the reason a district exists.

2. *Critical analysis.* Collection and analysis of vital data about all facets of the internal and the external environments of the school organization. It defines the status of a school organization and describes the future by combining forecasting results with status-check results.

3. *Assumptions.* A prediction of the events and conditions that are likely to influence the performance of a school organization, a division, or key individuals. Preparing planning assumptions is a form of forecasting. Assumptions are

concerned with what the future will look like and help bridge the gap between needs and action goals in the planning process.

4. *Components.* Means of grouping goals for the purposes of communication and management. All goals are assigned to a component, and each component consists of one or more goals.

5. *Objectives.* Statements of results that are measurable and that have time limitations. They describe the condition(s) a school organization wants to improve. The desired improvements are then translated into goals. Objectives are written for each goal. As objectives are met, goals are accomplished.

6. *Evaluation.* Statements of conditions that show evidence that an objective is satisfactorily achieved and procedures are developed for completing the evaluation. Each objective should be evaluated and the evaluation procedures should be developed at the time the objective is written.

7. *Action plans.* Actions to be taken that will help achieve the objectives. Each objective will have one or more activities. A due date, responsible person(s), and cost are significant parts of each activity.

8. *Monitoring.* System for assessing the status of activities, analyzing the results, and reporting outcomes.

9. *Stakeholders' involvement.* All stakeholders in a system (community, board, administrators, staff, and possibly students) are represented in the plan development.

10. *Linkage documents.* All documents in a system are aligned to the plan.

Another way a school district becomes rational is in establishing "best practices" and working toward paradigm shifts to bring this about. Few districts are systematically building in benchmarks of best practice.

Establishing an Integrated, Webbed
Management Structure: Premise Eight

One very important way in which systems thinking influences our school districts is to move our organizational structures into 21st-century management approaches. Senge (1990) suggests an integrated, webbed organizational structure. Such organizational structures are fluid and share power. Deming (1982), in one of his 14 points, indicates that we need to break down barriers between departments. People must work as a team to foresee problems in the organization and work together for continuous improvement.

We must make several changes in our school districts to bring this about. First, we must move away from the hierarchical, military style of management. Such organizational structures are usually top-down in command, disconnected, and fragmented. Competition is the focus, a muscle-bound approach of "do it my way or else." Most of our school systems use a hierarchical system that is typically paternalistic and dependent. The only purpose of such an organizational structure is to show who is hired and evaluated by whom.

Recently, site-based decision making has been an attempt to change the organizational structure to be more meaningful. However, such attempts seem to be failing. Changing a structure from top-down to bottom-up still represents a fragmented, linear approach to decision making. Neither are systemic.

Moving toward a shared approach to team decision making and using people, regardless of position, to solve problems, are components of systems thinking. A collaborative and affiliation approach to understanding the integration of people and functions is the focus—an inclusive web of people working together making decisions for the group. They function as a team to make decisions about the district. Such approaches can permeate all divisions, schools, and departments. They are best begun when the superintendent and board move top management into a webbed structure.

An illustration of the traditional approach versus a systems approach is shown in Figure 3.4.

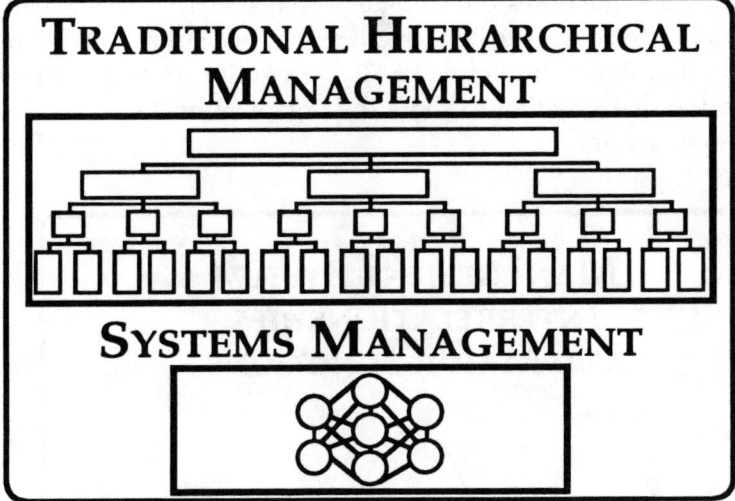

Figure 3.4

There are several advantages of the inclusive, webbed structure:

1. Flexibility without lowering morale—people are not primarily concerned with rank and position.
2. One can serve on various teams without worrying about whether the assignment is appropriate to status.
3. The inclusive, webbed structure takes full advantage of staff skills and talents.
4. It flattens the organization so that staff can be rotated, resulting in fewer promotions and demotions.
5. There is a greater flow of information.
6. There is more direct, free-flowing, integrated communication.

Most school districts using a flattened, webbed structure take advantage of cross-functional teams. Such interdependent teams cut across lines of authority and departments/schools/divisions. Integrated teams are constituted for a short period of time to accomplish a particular process improvement, project, or task across the system.

Figure 3.5 illustrates the Kyrene School District's (1992-1993) interrelationships and major functions. The organizational configuration is shown in Figure 3.6. These two illustrations can be laid on top of each other to show the organizational structure of the school system.

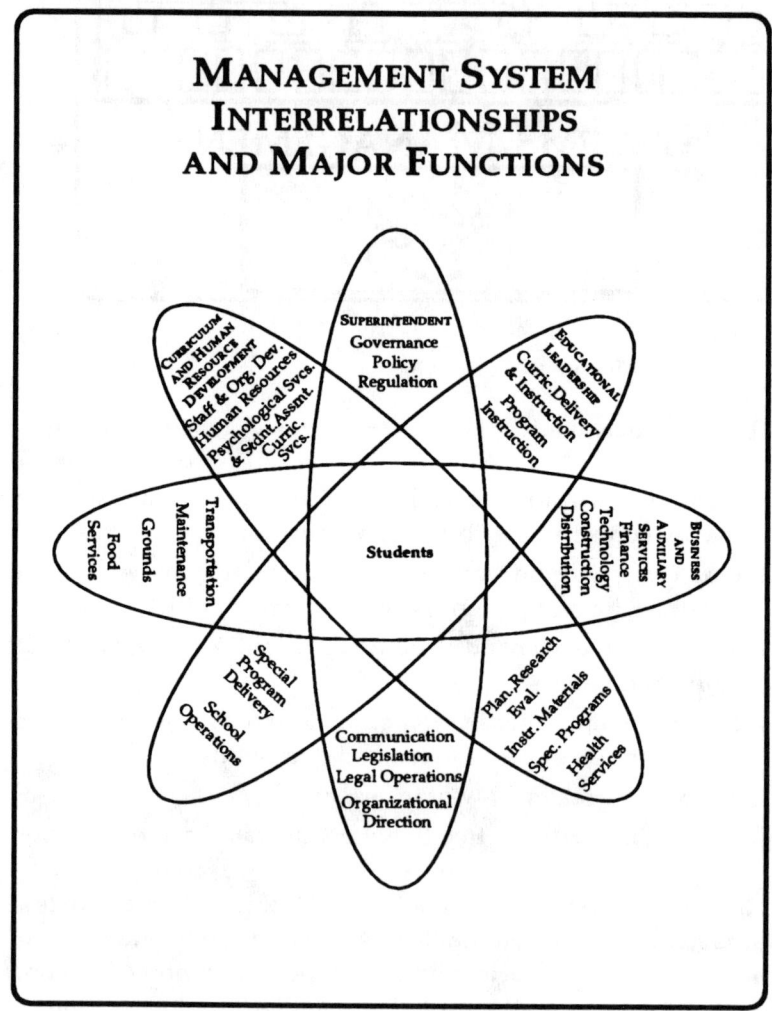

Figure 3.5

ORGANIZATIONAL CONFIGURATION

Figure 3.6

An equally important chart from the school system is the districtwide decision-making structure (see Figure 3.7). It shows the various teams and their relationships.

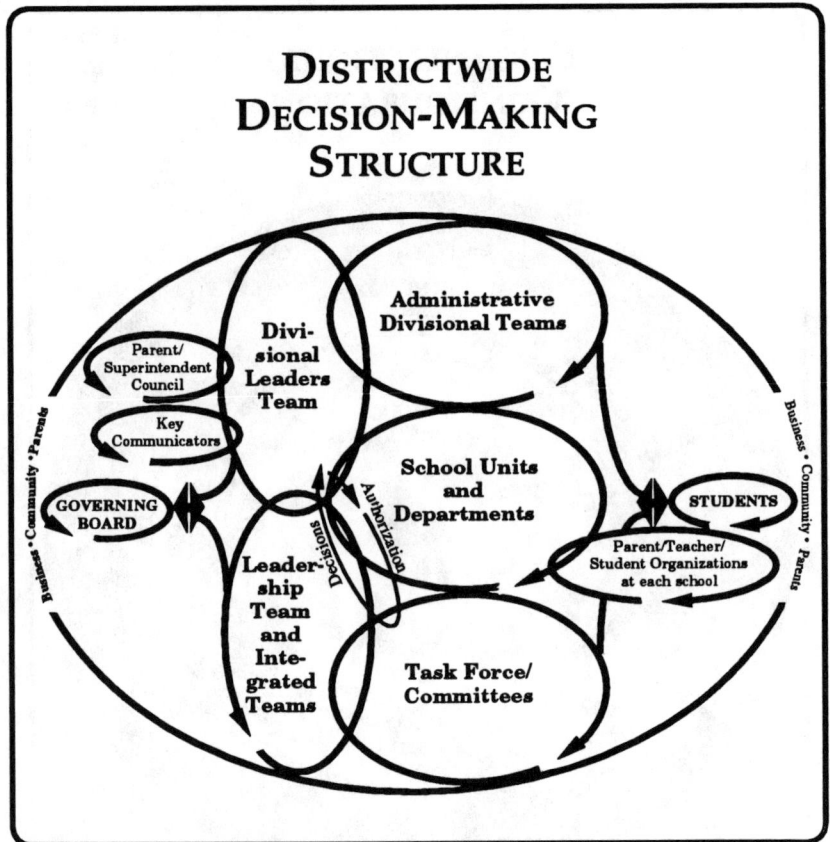

Figure 3.7

The district used the structure of adhocracy for major decisions to bring substantive changes to the organization. The task forces and committees made recommendations directly to the leadership team. In those cases where governance was involved, the decisions then flowed to the governing board.

Using an Adhocracy Approach to Management

An adhocracy approach is an effective way to increase the likelihood of innovative organizations. It is highly recommended as the way to bring about major changes in school districts. Waterman (1990) compares bureaucracy versus adhocracy. Bureaucracies are designed to carry out tomorrow what you are doing today. Adhocracy is a way of doing something different tomorrow than you are doing today. It is the use of temporary groups brought together to accomplish a particular task to effect change in the school district.

There are several critical attributes of an effective adhocracy (Waterman, 1990). An effective adhocracy

- Requires broad participation
- Cuts across conventional lines and boundaries
- Directly confronts poor communication
- Encourages a team effort
- Requires trust and integrity
- Minimizes mindless bureaucracy
- Works only when the leaders expect it to work

Any working group needs to know the degree of influence it has over a decision. Some superintendents and governing board members have made the mistake of giving a group authority for a decision and then reversing the group's recommendation. Even if leaders clearly request a recommendation, they must seldom reverse or change or send the decision back to the group. This means we have to be very clear initially about the parameters of the decision and have opportunities to influence the decision along the way. Otherwise, the entire approach to shared decision making can be nullified.

Being Clear about Participatory Versus Shared Decision Making

Many school districts have been participatory in nature for several years. Leaders have gathered input from members of the district and then decided on the direction to take. Or the leader calls together a team of people to collect input and then decides. A shared decision-making process calls for a different approach. In this case, either a consensus approach in which the leader is an equal member in the decision is taken, or the leader delegates the decision to a team designated to reach consensus on the problem.

Figure 3.8 provides a continuum of involvement that can help us when we create groups. Note the difference between participatory approaches and shared decision-making approaches.

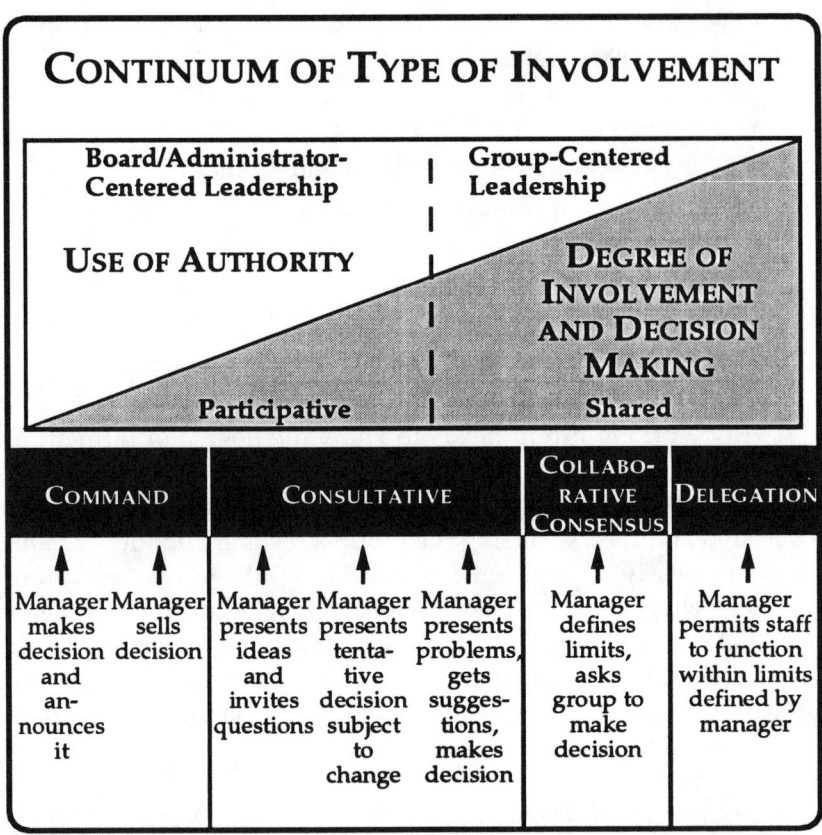

Figure 3.8

When we meet with a group, we need to be clear about our role. Another way of illustrating our role in relation to teams is shown in Figure 3.9. The dark circle is you.

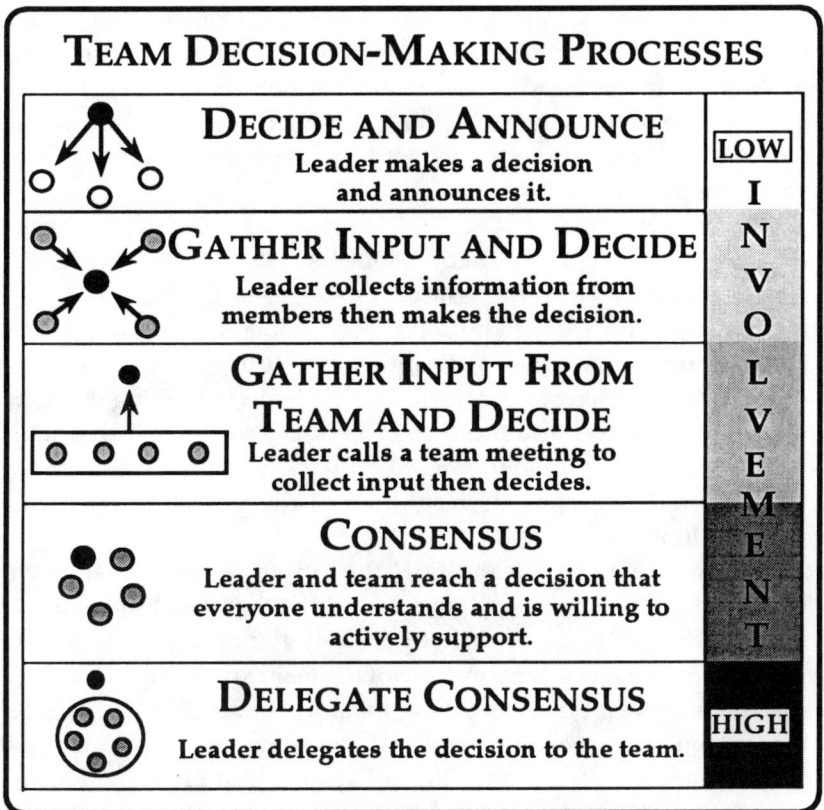

Figure 3.9

Implementing an Integrated, Webbed Structure

Moving a district to an interdependent structure is not easy. For years our staff and students have been comfortable in a dependency role, and we have enjoyed taking care of them. Quality leadership challenges us to become interdependent leaders. We share power and become equal colleagues with others to solve school systems' problems and to fulfill the mission.

For those of us who have used the paternalistic or benevolent dictator style, it will not be an easy transition (Downey, 1992). Like the Lone Ranger, we have been validated for taking charge of the problem, and staff and students are rescued. With a "Hi Ho Silver" we are off into the sunset and those left behind think we are wonderful. Actually, we have just kept them dependent on us to solve the problems.

Senge (1990) conveys several learning disabilities that come into play in this type of situation. One he calls "I am my position." As we move away from position power to influence power, we must work with those who have been dependent on our voice. Position power becomes a disability by stifling innovation. Another disability Senge discusses is the "illusion of taking charge." Often, we may fall into the trap of taking over when a district is facing a difficult problem. We are only fooling ourselves; "group think" usually can handle resolution of the problem better than we can alone.

Another learning disability is the "myth of the management team." This is when we say we are working together, but we really are not. Senge (1990) says that probably the only people we are fooling are ourselves. Staff outside of the team know quickly when a management team is not working in an integrated way. A management team is supposed to sort out the complex cross-functional issues that are critical to the school system. But often the leaders spend their time fighting for turf, avoiding anything that will make them look bad personally, and pretending that everyone is behind the team's collective decision. Later, disenfranchised team members may covertly interfere with the decision.

To become effective, we must assist employees and other stakeholders in recognizing the power that lies within each one of them. We need to provide them the authority to identify and act on their own initiative to correct common causes of variation—the source of most quality problems (Deming, 1991).

How can we encourage the stakeholders of the school systems to become teams with group synergy? And moreover, how can we move into a leadership role that brings about interdependency rather than dependency? It is hard. But it is an exciting journey when administrators, staff, parents, students, and external customers come together in a systemic way to fulfill the district's mission. Each member becomes a highly competent, best-in-the-field person working collaboratively with all the others—the dream team (Downey, 1992).

Focusing on Process Management in the Educational Arena: Premise Nine

A major focus of the quality movement is away from "bottom-line" thinking to focusing on the process. First, improving the process is the personal responsibility of each employee of the school system, and each person can influence the overall processes of the district. Administrators have a major role in improving the process and ensuring that every employee's contributions are used to improve the system. Each of us is charged to add value to the learning of children through our processes.

Emphasis in a quality system is on working on the methods—the processes. Scholtes (1988) stresses that we should not focus on the product but, rather, on building excellence into every aspect of the school district. Employees and management must work together in a partnership to bring about change. Using scientific approaches, we can solve problems and make improvements in the system together.

Deming's (1991) chain, as depicted in Figure 3.10, shows the relationship of process to product.

Deming has much to say about working on the process. One of his 14 points is to eliminate numerical quotas, and another is to do away with all slogans and exhortations that ask employees to work harder. Those organizations that have quotas will try to meet or exceed the quota at any cost, regardless of quality. We often see this happening in school districts when student achievement scores become targets. To "look good" on tests administered by the state or province, a district becomes test-driven. If these tests are not measuring the important learnings for students, the student customer is probably being harmed. Deming feels strongly that goals must focus on quality issues, not on the number produced.

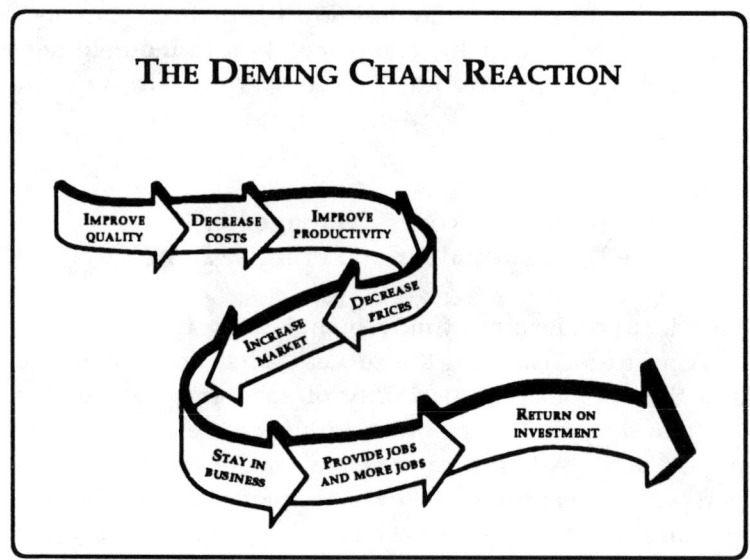

Figure 3.10

So, then, where should we put our focus? Sashkin and Kiser (1991) identify five quality checkpoints where processes can be improved. These processes are quality leverage points that flow like a stream. In a traditional model, the typical and often the only point of checking before giving the product or service to the customer is at Quality Checkpoint (QC) 2—the end of a process. Using all points focuses more on the customer, the supplier, and the process than on the product.

The following are Sashkin and Kiser's (1991) five quality check-points:

1. *User point.* First and foremost, we need to determine how well our service to our customers meets their needs and desires in the actual world setting. For our students, this would mean following them into society to see how well they are functioning and how well they believe their education helped them in society. Only when one knows customer

needs, wants, and expectations can transformation processes that will meet those desires be designed.

2. *Distribution point.* This checkpoint is the final inspection prior to customer use. This point has historically been the primary focus of quality control activities.

3. *Process of actual production or service delivery.* The use of statistical process control here to assess quality in the process becomes very important. Here we should focus on improving the few critical elements that will have the greatest effect. Using best practices in our school district with a focus on curriculum and instructional delivery would be valuable.

4. *Incoming quality assurance.* As we receive our products from suppliers and vendors, we should check the quality of the product. How does this fit into education? In the noninstructional areas, this is easy to translate—instructional materials, facilities, and so on. It could also include new staff by diagnosing their competence and specifying areas for professional growth. Mainly, we need to diagnose our students for their talents and knowledge to better differentiate our learning opportunities for them.

5. *Supply point.* This checkpoint becomes very important in our instructional arena. The idea here is to work with suppliers and vendors to improve their products and services before they reach us. This is easy to understand when we are talking about working with architects to improve our buildings or with book suppliers to ensure that we have a better instructional resource. However, the most important translation is to work with parents who are the providers of the children with whom we work. Working with parents will help them to prepare their children before they come to our schools, and while they are in our schools.

Only school districts that manage each of the five quality checkpoints effectively, as part of a complete, continuous, and constant process, will successfully attain quality for all functions of the school system—governance, curriculum, instructional methods, staffing patterns, personnel issues, and budgeting.

Identifying Variation and Its Implications in Educational Settings: Premise Ten

Understanding variation is one of Deming's (1991) four areas of profound knowledge. Variation will always occur in all aspects of life. We need to know what the variation tells us about our work and about people. He suggests that we chart the variance.

It was Shewhart who first recognized the importance of understanding and measuring variability in a process (Sashkin & Kiser, 1991). Use of some of the quality tools serves the purpose of studying variation by:

1. Helping to describe and understand a work activity—a process
2. Determining when the data do not fit a normal distribution, and by
3. Helping to see how we can tighten up this distribution so that there is less variation

Deming (1991) points out two mistakes that are frequently made in attempts to improve results. Both are considered tampering. A mistake frequently made is to react to an outcome as if it came from a special cause, when actually it came from common causes of variation (often inherent). The other mistake is to treat an outcome as it if came from common causes of variation, when actually it came from a special cause—something unusual happens.

First, we want to find and eliminate the special causes of variation and bring them into a state of statistical control. Second, we need to work on improving the processes by reducing common causes of variation—causes that still exist when the process is in statistical control.

Common-cause problems are recurrent. They must be resolved by changing some component of the process. Deming (1991) contends the following:

- Rework will not help except as a temporary measure.
- Contingency plans will not work because the problems are recurring rather than being one-time events.

- Telling people to try harder will not work because the problem is inherent to the process, not the employees.
- Giving people new tools, changing the procedures, or changing the environment might help.

It is the responsibility of the person who owns the process to reduce common-cause problems.

With respect to special causes, Deming (1991) suggests that once recognized, they can usually be prevented or dealt with by a contingency plan. Process redesign is not the most cost-effective way to deal with special-cause problems, which are one-time events.

It is our responsibility to recognize variation in a service and to determine whether it is the result of common or special causes.

Variation is unavoidable. Teachers and students have differing talents, different styles, and like different things. Deming (1991) says that we must understand variation, or we may make decisions that tamper with the school system. Understanding variation statistically allows us to know how a stable school system is performing.

One way to deal with variation is to improve the processes that may be influencing the lower limits of the common causes. This is often done in school systems by working with those students who are not in special-category programs but are "lost in the middle." Lazotte (1986) asserts that by taking the 10 lowest students in every class and by developing an individual education plan for them, we can probably decrease much of the variation. This reduction in variation can be illustrated as shown in Figure 3.11.

We can develop strategies for improving the common-cause variation (see Figure 3.12). We can also work on special-cause variation (see Figure 3.13).

Figure 3.14 is an example of combining a way of looking at both common causes and special causes to improve the productivity of students gradually.

We might find that we would use very different strategies if we began to examine many of the things we now label as special causes and find out that they are common causes. For example, there is research to suggest that we are placing far too many

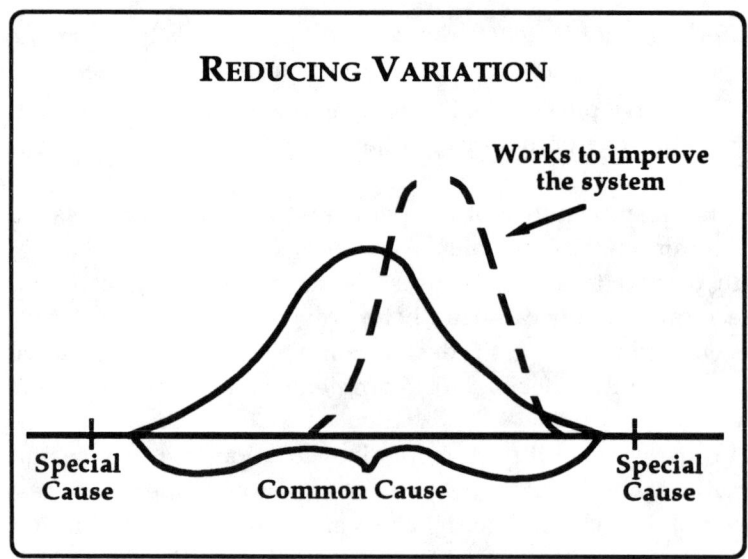

Figure 3.11

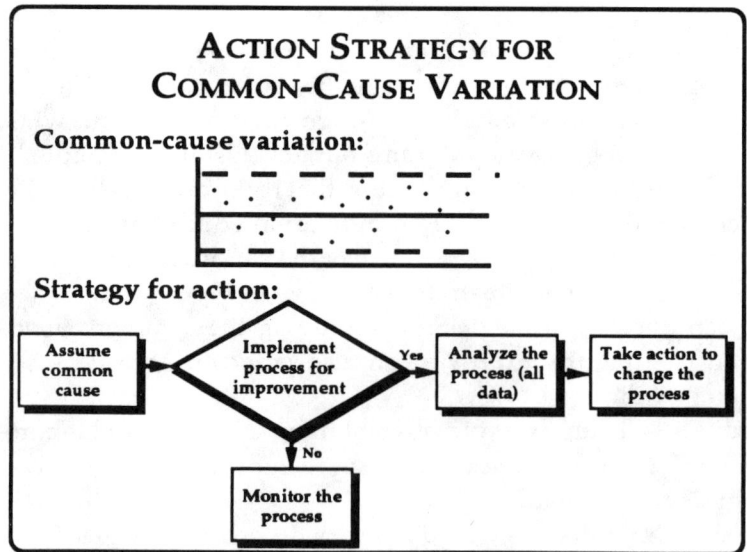

Figure 3.12

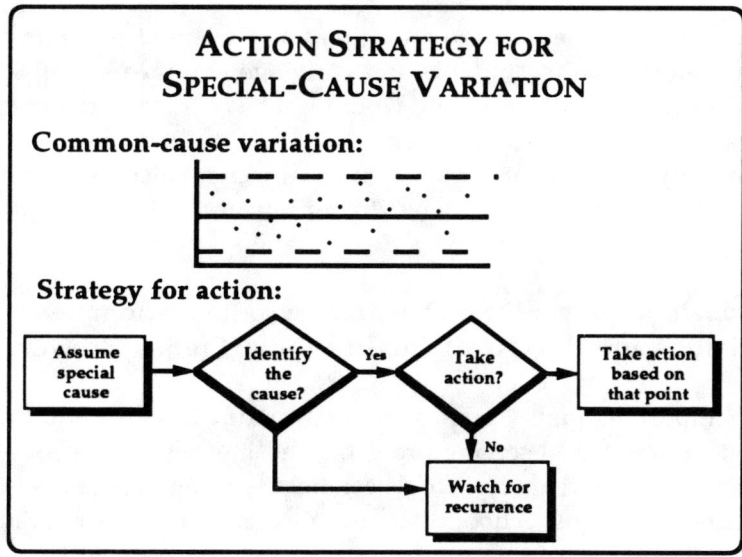

Figure 3.13

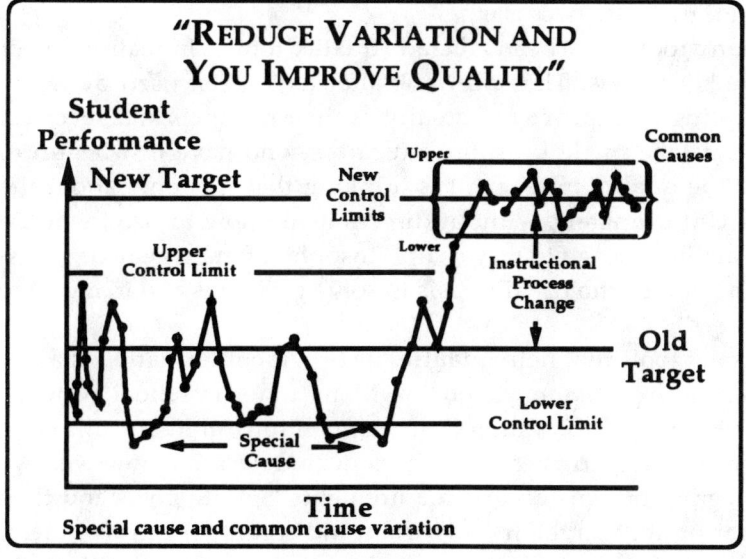

Figure 3.14

children in special education and gifted and talented programs. The nonpromotion of students and early-age entrance are other problematic areas. We probably would not have transitional first grades if we understood variation.

Studying the concept of variation in our school districts could have major effects on the way we do our business.

Encouraging a Data Orientation to Educational Decisions and the Use of Quality Tools: Premise Eleven

An important quality premise of the structure leverage point is to be data oriented in solving problems and improving processes. Using planning and analysis tools can help to bring a database to our school decisions. School districts collect a lot of information, but is it the right information? We need to determine what we need to know—for what purpose—and then collect and analyze the data we need. Deming (1991) talks about asking the right question to figure out which sort of data, which numbers, and which figures are necessary.

Many tools have been labeled "quality tools." In reality, few of the tools are new. They are tools that have been used by many attempting to improve the quality of their products and services.

A mistake made by some educators who have just begun to study the quality movement is thinking that it is only about the tools. Unfortunately, without directions on how to use them the tools are just tools. Quality is a philosophy of management focusing on people who use the tools to solve problems and to improve processes.

Use of tools that help quantify or provide information is a key element in process improvement. Many times in school systems, we use our intuition rather than being empirical in our thinking. We must be data driven. Data help us to determine how well we are meeting our customers' requirements. Setting goals and then measuring that target are important indicators for improvement. Good use of tools tracks the use of resources and how efficiently they are used (Latta & Downey, 1994).

To deal with variation in systems, the quality movement has a process called statistical process control (SPC). This is a method for determining the cause of variation based on a statistical analysis of the problem. It uses probability theory to control and to improve processes. First, the problem is identified. Then quantifiable data are used for analysis. This provides a reference point or a data baseline. Once the problem is identified and common and special causes are determined, a cause-and-effect analysis is developed. From this, additional data are collected and statistically analyzed, and corrective action is taken.

An entire book in this series is devoted to the quality tools and their applications (Latta & Downey, 1994). This section will briefly define some of these tools.

Introducing the Seven Old Tools

The first set of tools is known as the seven old quality tools. These are illustrated in Figures 3.15 through 3.21.

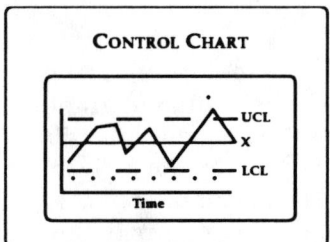

Control chart. A chart showing the sequential or time-related performance of a process that is used to determine when the process is operating in and out of statistical control—using control limits defined on the chart.

Figure 3.15

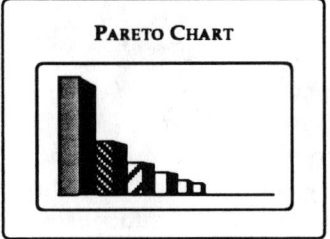

Pareto chart. A type of bar chart, prioritized in descending order from left to right, used to identify the vital few opportunities for improvement. Eighty percent of the problems come from 20% of the reasons.

Figure 3.16

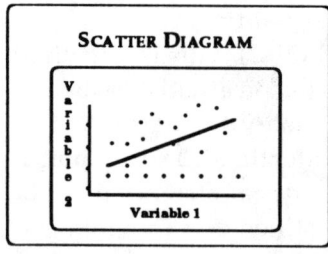

Figure 3.17

Scatter diagram. Chart in which one variable is plotted against another to determine if there is a correlation between the two variables. Comparisons can then be made to determine degree of correlation.

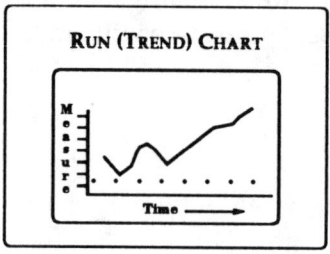

Figure 3.18

Run (trend) chart. A graphic plot versus time of a measurable characteristic of a process. It shows a running tally over time. Use when you want to know if there are critical times when something is occurring.

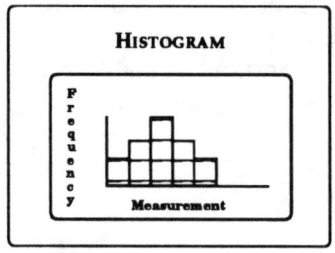

Figure 3.19

Histogram. A bar (column) graph that shows the frequency distribution of data collected on a given variable. The height of each column displays the frequency (number) of a given measurement.

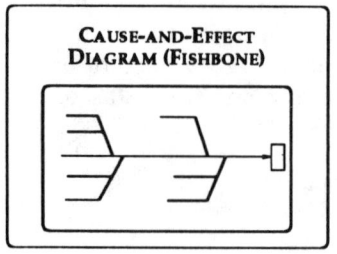

Figure 3.20

Fishbone diagram (cause-and-effect diagram, Ishikawa diagram). A structured form of brainstorming that graphically shows the relationship of possible causes and subcauses to an identified effect or problem.

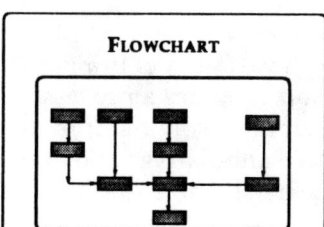

Figure 3.21

Flowchart. A chart that uses symbols to represent the input from suppliers, the sequential work activities, the decisions to be made, and the output to the customer. A flowchart is a visual way of charting a process from beginning to end.

Introducing Seven Planning Tools

The tools used to help in planning continuous improvement are depicted in Figures 3.22 through 3.28.

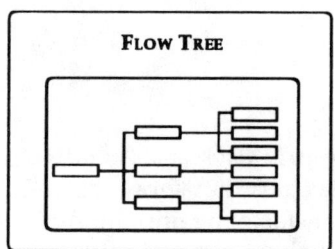

Figure 3.22

Flow tree. This is a planning tool used to graph a thinking process linearly and logically. It breaks down issues into identifiable components or action items that, when accomplished in sequence, yield attainment of the goal.

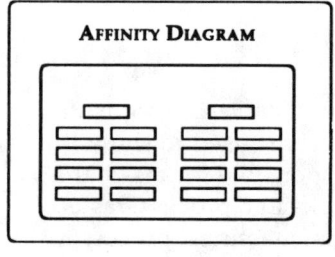

Figure 3.23

Affinity diagram. This is a planning tool used to group complex, apparently unrelated, data into natural and meaningful groups. Ideas are grouped according to their natural relationships.

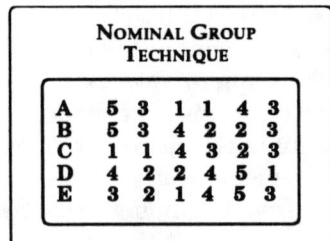

Figure 3.24

Nominal group technique. This planning tool is a variation of brainstorming and provides a process for group problem solving. It identifies creative alternatives and clarifies the most viable ideas.

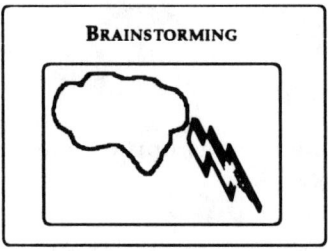

Figure 3.25

Brainstorming. An idea-generation technique that uses group interaction to generate many ideas in a short period of time. It stimulates creativity and encourages group participation.

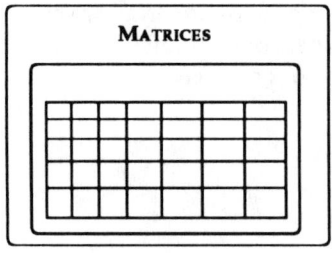

Figure 3.26

Matrices (matrix diagrams). A matrix is a simple chart that shows correlation of one factor against another. It can easily be combined with other tools such as the flow tree diagram to create powerful planning.

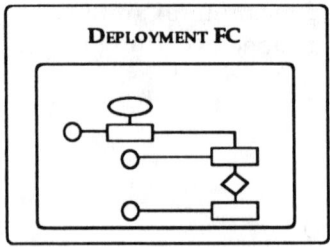

Figure 3.27

Deployment flowchart. A sophisticated flowchart used to show the people responsible for tasks, the flow of tasks in a process, tasks, documents, meetings, processes, decision, and assistance points.

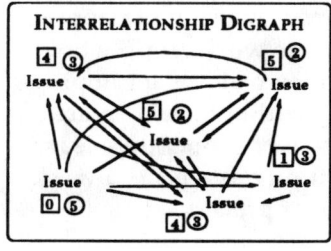

Interrelationship digraph (relations diagram). A planning tool that is a pictorial representation of the cause-and-effect relationships among the elements of a problem or issue. It is used for examining complex problems.

Figure 3.28

Introducing a Few More Tools

Several additional tools are used by quality experts. Seven are introduced in this section (see Figures 3.29 through 3.35).

<table>
<tr><td>

FORCE-FIELD ANALYSIS

ANALYSIS QUESTION: What are the driving and restraining forces that impact your organization's progress toward implementing Total Quality Management?

DRIVING FORCES →	←RESTRAINING FORCES

</td></tr>
</table>

Force-field analysis. A list identifying driving and restraining forces that must be overcome before the desired outcome can be effected. This analysis is accomplished through a group creative-thinking process.

Figure 3.29

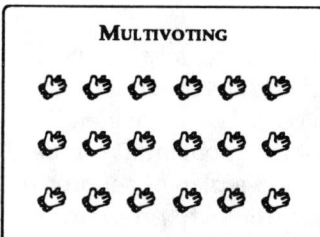

Multivoting. A technique for taking a large number of group-generated items and narrowing the list. Use multivoting when you want to limit the number of options, issues, problems, or solutions.

Figure 3.30

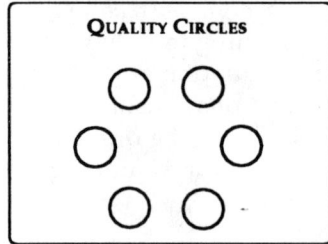

Figure 3.31

Quality circles. A group of people from the same work group who focus attention on ideas for improving quality within their own area. This is a type of cooperative learning opportunity as well as a work improvement process.

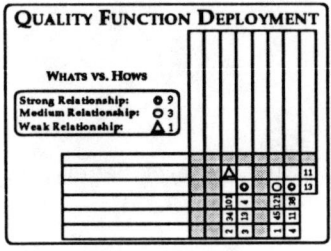

Figure 3.32

Quality function deployment (QFD). A matrix using tasks to achieve certain characteristics. The purpose is to identify and strengthen critical processes. It is a means of examining the needs of external customers.

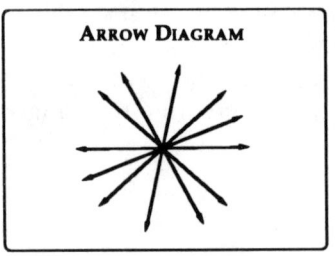

Figure 3.33

Arrow diagram. A management and planning tool used to develop a time-sequential plan for implementing improvement projects. Relationships and time lines are shown.

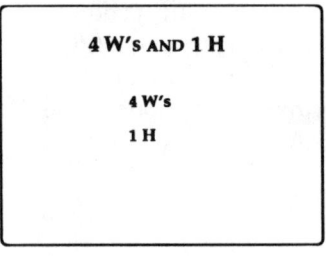

Figure 3.34

4 W's and 1 H—Who, what, when, where, and how. A useful tool to help develop an objective and a concise statement of the problem. It can be used to develop a plan of action to suggest resolutions to problems or improvement processes.

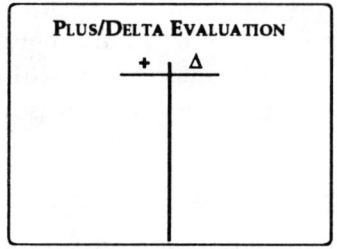

Figure 3.35

Plus/delta evaluation. A technique used for critiquing group sessions or meetings that identifies the areas that made the session successful and the areas that need improvement.

Several additional tools are not included in this chapter. As we move into integrated, collaborative, shared decision making, there are a host of tools to be used. These include team-building strategies, collaboration techniques, consensus approaches, and problem-solving techniques.

Summary

This chapter focused on those quality premises in the Quality Fit Framework that influence the structure of school districts. Systems thinking, optimization, and integrated organizational structures lead school districts toward a process for continuous improvement.

Key Terms and Concepts

Adhocracy approach to management. A strategy that uses temporary groups brought together to accomplish improvement.

Bureaucracy approach. Applying today's strategies and solutions tomorrow regardless of the fit with new challenges.

Common cause. Normal variation typically considered two standard deviations from the norm.

Delta. A process in which there is no added value.

Rational organization. An organization that connects its activities to attain its goals and that relates its internal activities to its purposes.

School system disabilities. Dysfunctions within a school or school system that preclude success, for example, belief that the enemy is "out there"; people are the problem, not their interactions with organizational structures and variables; and problems are isolated, not systemic.

Special cause. Unusual variation from the norm.

Systems thinking. Thinking of the organization or system as a network of functions or activities within the organization that must work together to achieve its aim.

Webbed structure. Organizational structures that are fluid and share power throughout the organization.

References

Deming, W. E. (1982). *Out of the crisis.* Cambridge: MIT Press.

Deming, W. E. (1991, March). *A system of profound knowledge.* Participant material distributed at the Quality Seminar, Santa Clara, CA.

Downey, C. J. (1992, September). Can the Lone Ranger join the dream team? *Quality Network News.* Arlington, VA: American Association of School Administrators.

English, F. (1987). *Curriculum management for schools, colleges, business.* Springfield, IL: Charles C Thomas.

English, F. (1988). *Curriculum auditing.* Lancaster, PA: Technomic.

Kyrene School District. (1992-1993). *Management structure of the Kyrene district.* Tempe, AZ.

Latta, R., & Downey, C. J. (1994). *Tools for achieving TQE.* Thousand Oaks, CA: Corwin.

Lazotte, R. (1986, January). *Effective schools strategies.* Outcomes Based Workshop, Phoenix, AZ.

Merriam-Webster's collegiate dictionary. (1993). Springfield, MA: Merriam-Webster.

Sashkin, M., & Kiser, K. (1991). *Total quality management.* Seabrook, NY: Ducochon.

Scholtes, P. R. (1988). *The team handbook.* Madison, WI: Joiner.

Senge, P. M. (1990). *The fifth discipline.* New York: Doubleday.

Waterman, R. H., Jr. (1990). *Adhocracy: The power to change.* New York: W. W. Norton.

✦ 4 ✦

Building Meaningful Interpersonal Relationships

The third leverage point in which we can make a major impact in our districts is in the area of interpersonal relationships or the dynamics of the relationships among people. The business of our school districts is people working together with students and other stakeholders for the purpose of gaining and sharing knowledge and experience both socially and intellectually. In order for the process of learning to be effective, we must seek to open up the classrooms and the schools to each other and to the public we serve. No longer can a school focus solely on the teacher instructing in the classroom. We must take a more universal view in which the entire educational workforce is committed to an educated society.

What this means is that in developing a mission and a vision for our schools, we must involve all stakeholders in the educational community. Although teachers' interactions with students are key, we must recognize the important roles support staff and administrators play in helping teachers to do their job. The parents, students, and other community members are our customers. They, too, desire to be directly involved in the course schools are taking in the future. We need a transformation of our school systems from a traditional culture to one that is more flexible and innovative. To do this, we must mobilize our entire workforce and coordinate their efforts with those of the larger community. As this occurs, a new environment of trust, openness, and understanding must be forged among us to allow the energy of conflict to be managed to our advantage.

This can occur if we begin to recognize the changes that must be made in our interpersonal relationships and culture to promote this new cooperation. In this chapter, we explore interpersonal relationships and their impact on the transformation of school systems. Seven quality premises within the Quality Fit Framework are linked to the leverage point of interpersonal relationships:

- Mobilizing the workers
- Working in collaborative, interdependent ways
- Bringing about shared values and beliefs
- Understanding motivation
- Faults of systems rather than people
- Providing for a community of learners
- Constant communication and feedback

Mobilizing All Workers Toward the Aims of the System: Premise Twelve

Employees in quality organizations have the authority to identify problems and to act on their own initiative to correct common causes of variation—the source of most quality problems. Scholtes (1988) believes quality leadership creates an environment of *all one team*. The establishment of a team environment is not an easy task. A transformation in management style and organizational culture is often necessary before barriers interfering with teamwork can be breached.

It is not unusual for employees in school districts to work in a fragmented, isolated manner, much like a team of gymnasts whose individual performance counts toward an overall score. The team does well if each of the athletes performs well in his or her separate and isolated events, such as the floor exercise, uneven parallel bars, and vaulting. In this arena, there is no call for interdependence among team members to secure the gold medal, just strong individual performance.

However, if we were to look at a school system embracing the idea of quality, a different picture would unfold. We would see employees mobilizing themselves much like a team of basketball players. Highly interdependent, these individuals must interact as one as they choreograph plays and precisely position themselves to receive a pass and relay that pass to a teammate who is then able to avoid a defender and to score.

Interdependence has a higher value than independence (Covey, 1989). In order for an organization such as a school system to become a truly high-performing team, the barriers that impede interdependence must be dismantled. The mobilization throughout an organization of teams of employees who have a sense of efficacy occurs through the creation of an environment that avoids behaviors that encourage the stratification or the isolation of employees and groups of employees. Many of our current organizational and personal behaviors promote the idea that one group of employees is more important than another. For example, support staff members in many school districts feel like "second-class citizens." In taking a close look at our behaviors, this perception is easy to understand.

Other examples can be seen in the behaviors between management and employees and between site management and central management. Power struggles, autocratic behaviors, and "parking lot conversations," where negative hypotheses concerning motivations are shared among members of individual employee groups, cause feelings of distrust and encourage isolation. Such behaviors give credence to the belief held by some that a caste system exists within educational organizations.

As we create a quality environment where all workers are mobilized toward the purpose of an organization, we must seek to reflect quality beliefs consistently in our behaviors. For example,

- Employees in an organization are all part of one team working together to accomplish a common mission.
- Teams create change, solve problems, and make improvements as they strive to accomplish an organization's mission.
- Employees have a sense of efficacy and become self-responsible and accountable.

- An environment must be established where fear and alienation are eliminated.

Strategies for Mobilizing our Employees

What actions will mobilize a group of isolated, independent employees into a team of coordinated, interdependent employees? First, employees must have equal access to training experiences in which they can participate together. This training must model interdependency and cut across the divergent functions within an organization. Facilitation skill training is critical as the role of manager changes from director to facilitative leader (Downey, 1993). Training needs to include basic beliefs about quality incorporating the quality premises identified in this book. An understanding of the uses of quality tools and processes must be gained by employees and incorporated into their actions as they work together to solve real problems in the school district.

Second, an environment of mutual respect among employees who contribute to the purpose of the organization through the accomplishment of different functions must be established. Equitable treatment needs to occur in the area of policy development, and fair and market-sensitive compensation standards and processes are important factors that must be established. A sense of fairness and appreciation should also be reflected by developing regard for all employee contributions to the common purpose of the organization.

Finally, cross-functional teams where individual team members have adequate access to one another, other teams, available resources, and a shared information base that will allow them to make decisions at the lowest level possible in an organization must be established.

Encouraging Interdependent Workers: Premise Thirteen

Once an organization has initiated the mobilization of its workforce through empowerment strategies, it must concurrently encourage interdependent behaviors among its workers.

Workers are highly sensitive to change in an organization. Systemic improvements should be implemented by teams of collaboratively cooperative staff who work interdependently to carry out their duties. This sense of interdependency must begin to be reflected in the behaviors of all employees so that it becomes part of the organizational culture.

An interdependent culture is exemplified by cooperative, noncompetitive employees. These individuals view themselves as being members of one team and are clear in their vision of how their activities contribute to the aim of the organization. Each individual has a sense of personal responsibility and pride in workmanship. As in the mobilization of workers, Deming's (1992) process of breaking down barriers among staff continues to be encouraged.

Covey (1989) has a clear vision about the concepts of dependency, independence, and interdependence. School systems have traditionally had a dependent focus. Administrators were highly autocratic and paternalistic in their management styles, believing that they knew more than the employees they were entrusted to supervise and to manage. They reflected a theory X (Ouchi, 1981) management style, which states that employees are basically unmotivated and in need of constant inspection and direction to accomplish the goals of the organization. This creates an environment of dependency that satisfies many employees until such time as their needs are not met.

Interestingly, as education employees realized their frustrations within a dependent system, they sought empowerment through advocacy organizations such as the American Federation of Teachers and the National Education Association, whose systems of field representatives and top-down leadership also created dependency.

Employees began to feel like victims of cruel overseers whose only recourse was some sort of dramatic, systemic junta where paternalistic administrators would be replaced by equally paternalistic employee leaders. Employee groups that sought their independence in this manner were met, for the most part, with an organizational response of autocratic power strategies to maintain authority. The energies of the organization were diverted from the common mission of providing excellent educational services to children to a highly competitive power struggle between labor and management.

Seeking independence through further dependent behavior is not the road to interdependence. Instead, it creates an environment of competition that leads to the diffusion of energy away from the mission of an organization.

Using Covey's Seven Habits

Covey (1989) describes the road to interdependence as paved first with private victories leading to independence and then public victories that lead to interdependence through the acquisition of "habits" that manifest themselves as consistent behaviors. The first three habits, as described by Covey, are "Be proactive," "Begin with the end in mind, " and "Put first things first."

In his proactive model, Covey (1989) illustrates life awareness, imagination, conscience, and independent will as subsets of our freedom to choose. We can choose to be reactive, such as resorting to the primordial survival instincts of fighting or fleeing, or we may choose to be proactive by identifying and clarifying our core values without becoming defensive, protective, or offensive. As we deal with conflict or divergency of culture or perspective, we have the freedom to choose our responses to those stimuli.

Beginning with the end in mind is a habit that is primarily focused on the concept of leadership. Leaders provide a direction, a purpose, and a feeling of family, whereas management is more concerned with control, efficiency, and rules. Often, we become consumed with the setting and the achievement of goals before we have established a clear sense of purpose and clarification of values. By being proactive and using our imagination and conscience, we can vividly visualize our ultimate potential. In this way, we can rewrite our outdated scripts and reprogram the antediluvian tapes that have been placed within us through experience and may be erroneously driving our behaviors.

Covey (1989) speaks of the center of our lives being the source of our security, guidance, wisdom, and power, which in turn will empower our ability to be proactive while giving us a sense of congruency and harmony as we look toward our visions of the future. As one way to establish a personal mind sight of an end, he suggests we begin with the development of a personal mission statement.

Putting first things first is the "Just do it" part of reaching independence as one seeks interdependence. It is the practice of self-management that impacts a person's personal and professional life. According to Covey (1989), leadership is a right-brain activity, whereas management is affected by the left side of the brain. Management involves prioritization of activities that focus on maintaining and improving relationships and accomplishing results. It is about learning to discipline oneself and being able to say a pleasant "No" to invitations that do not fit into one's priorities.

After attaining independence through the private victory of mastering the first three habits, we can begin the task of developing the final three habits that will lead us to public victory and interdependence. These habits are "Think win/win," "Seek first to understand, then to be understood," and "Synergize."

The concept of win/win is one in which all parties involved in an issue or problem arrive at a mutually satisfactory resolution. Irving Goldaber (1982) called it "New promise," wherein all parties could obtain something as opposed to compromise, wherein all parties had to give up something. Deming (1982) describes it as innovation. In any event, win/win is the creation of a third alternative that seeks a better solution to a problem.

"Listening with respect" is another way to phrase Covey's (1989) concept of seek first to understand, then to be understood. Seeking first to take in fully and to understand another's perspective prior to presenting one's own is a highly sophisticated skill that requires incredible self-discipline. How often have we found ourselves formulating a defense or rebuttal before a speaker has finished verbalizing his or her thought? And then there's the case where we have actually interrupted a person to voice our own perspective.

Synergizing is the final habit one must master to be truly interdependent with others. Simply put, synergy means, "The whole is greater than the sum of its parts."

Covey (1989) emphasizes another belief that will assist us in sustaining our energy and zest for life. "Sharpen the saw" is a habit most of us seem to put on the back burner of our helter-skelter lives. It reflects the concept of wellness and self-renewal both in the physical and spiritual self. People on high-performing teams make time for such experiences and incorporate them into their weekly activities.

Creating a Shared Culture of Values and Beliefs Within the Organization: Premise Fourteen

How leaders facilitate a culture of shared values is an important relationship variable and an important quality premise. The foundation of the culture must be built on a solid environment of fairness, openness, trust, and respect for the dignity of others. Clear standards or norms for behaviors and conflict management must be collaboratively developed and incorporated into the organizational culture. These standards should be developed concurrently and in concert with the organization's endeavors to mobilize and assist employees in becoming interdependent. Sashkin and Kiser (1991) support the creation and sustaining of a culture based on shared beliefs and have identified these goals as important ingredients in the development of a quality-driven organization.

Most individuals can articulate what they value. In the arena of relationships, most can reach consensus on the golden rule, "Treat others as we would want others to treat us." The forming of what people say they value into statements of beliefs that will drive the development of an interdependent value system is relatively easy compared to the integration of behaviors that reflect those articulated values and beliefs. In other words, it is much easier to "Talk the talk" than it is to "Walk the talk."

Environmental factors that appear again and again in organizations are the concepts of trust, openness, and honesty. These are values to which individuals within an organization aspire but often fail to model in their behaviors. Ineffective communication due to poor listening and insufficient questioning for clarity may lead to misinterpretation, misunderstanding, anger, and hurt feelings, resulting in an erosion of trust.

Hidden agendas, unilateral positioning, and special interests that are exemplified by behaviors indicative of secretiveness, inflexibility, inconsistency, or manipulation can impact perceptions of honesty or ethics. Closed posture, flip comments, artificial barriers, and a lack of rapport contribute to a closed environment where ideas, feelings, and creative thinking are not shared.

The development of an understanding of an effective team environment is the first step in developing interrelationships among group members that will allow for management of the whirlpools and winds of the inevitable conflicts that will arise among individuals in an organization. Once these logical norms are integrated into an organization's behaviors and become part of its culture, conflict management becomes second nature to the people within the culture.

Helping Create the Culture

Deming's (1982) 14th point regarding quality is *take action to accomplish the transformation.* The transformation of an organization from a traditionally based culture to a quality culture or from being able merely to articulate quality beliefs into acting on them is a difficult task. First, it is helpful to understand the concept of transformation as it relates to reformation or conformation.

Reformation or conformation, like rearranging the deck chairs on the Titanic or shedding one's outside layer, uses much energy but results in essentially the same outcome as if no action at all had been taken. Transformation, however, uses energy to recreate something totally different.

When we talk about the transformation of an organization's culture from a traditional to a quality paradigm, we are talking about purposeful, systemic change that completely alters the very being of that organization.

Understanding Worker Motivation: Premise Fifteen

Leaders must take the time to become aware of how people are motivated and develop strategies to assist them in seeking motivation intrinsically as opposed to extrinsically. This is one of the most powerful premises of the Quality Fit Framework. Employees should be encouraged to become self-motivated in the areas of skill improvement, new skill development, and quality improvement ideas and processes. Any organizational reward should be gained from this premise and not be generated on performance. Most school reward and recognition systems are based on extrinsic motivation. Major changes will be required in school districts to implement the motivation premise.

Divergence in the personalities within a group struggling to become a team can have a deleterious effect on the group unless it is understood and properly facilitated. A leader who is sensitive to these differences has an opportunity to assist group members in transforming their need for extrinsic praise, rewards, and motivation to meet their self-esteem and worth needs to learning how to have these needs met intrinsically. By honoring individuals with trust, the leader can empower them in becoming innovative. As a person becomes innovative and divergent in his or her thinking, he or she will begin to make systems improvements.

Recognizing Faults in the System and Remedying Them Through Innovative Solutions: Premise Sixteen

Fix the problem, not the blame. Rather than believing that most problems are a result of employee behavior, the quality movement recognizes that most failures are attributable to system problems. Process improvement becomes the focus, not individual culpability. The transformed organization seeks to identify the core problems within a system and then interdependently develops innovative solutions for problem resolution.

Performance evaluation of school employees provides a perfect example of an inspection model that focuses on the individual performance of an employee as opposed to the performance of the system. Traditionally, educational employees have been evaluated with a checklist of observable or demonstrable traits, characteristics, objectives, or indicators. A teacher who could demonstrate the various components of Madeline Hunter's (1982) Effective Instruction Model was considered to be an acceptable performer. Custodians or secretaries who could demonstrate timeliness, initiative, and a strong work ethic would have their employment renewed for another year. Administrators who could control their employees, manage parents, and enforce procedures were likewise considered to be performing at an acceptable level.

If evidence existed that any of these individuals was not living up to district standards, an individualized performance improvement plan was developed so that their lack of skill could be remediated. And, if they could not remediate their deficiency, they were either removed from the system, transferred to another location, or ignored.

Inspection systems such as these are often required by outdated state or provincial statutes. Point 3 of Deming's (1986) 14 points is *cease dependence on mass inspection.* A school transforming its evaluation system from an individualized inspection model to a systems model subscribes to the Deming concept of improving the process not the person. Glaser (1990) suggests that when a lead-manager (instead of a boss-manager) works with an employee during the evaluation process, over time the employee's evaluation of himself or herself is more valid than the supervisor's. He indicates that the goal of the supervisor is to teach the employee to be self-reflective and personally responsible for his or her work.

In many cases, school districts are working with employees to develop a systems approach toward evaluating and resolving performance problems. Instead of inspecting individuals, these districts are beginning to develop procedures to analyze systems problems and to make the necessary changes to remedy the situation.

It is important to note that this premise applies to students, too.

Providing for a Community of Learners: Premise Seventeen

Establishing a community of learners is achieved by providing ongoing education and training to internal and external customers as well as learning teams in a continuous effort to improve the system. Deming (1982) has identified a worker's education and training as critical to the well-being of the employee and the organization. Senge (1990) identified "community of learners" as one of his disciplines.

Over the past decade, school systems have begun to realize the value of staff and stakeholder development. However, we often find that development opportunities are available only for some of the employees and only in a fragmentaed way. Moreover, when budget cuts are needed, the area of professional and stakeholder growth and learning is often the first budget area to be excised. Business and industry have long recognized that without re-sources being invested in employee growth the company is not adequately prepared to interact successfully in the long-term mar-ket.

Deming (1982) stresses the importance of training throughout his 14 principles of quality management:

- Point 5: Improve constantly and forever the system of pro-duction and service.
- Point 6: Institute training.
- Point 13: Institute a vigorous program of education and retraining.
- Point 14: Take action to accomplish the transformation.

Points 5 and 14 do not specifically address staff development and training, but the concept of learning is embedded within their words. Whenever teams are actively engaged in constant im-provement and taking action for change, they are learning the task at hand from one another and from their own actions. Staff develop-ment need not always take the form of a seminar or a workshop. It does not have to be in a classroom with a formal curriculum and a teacher. The notion of continuous learning is one that every team and individual in an organization must strive to make a part of his or her core being and practice in his or her behaviors every minute of every day.

Establishing the Importance of Communication and Feedback: Premise Eighteen

The final premise of the Quality Fit Framework involves communication and feedback. More and more, quality leaders are pointing out the need for ongoing communication among managers and workers to effect improvement in the organization (Joiner, 1985). Important to communication is feedback within and among units of the organization. Senge (1990) speaks of the difference between dialogue and discussion. Dialogue happens when we are willing to suspend our thinking in order to be open to one another's perspectives. Covey (1989) addresses communication in his fifth habit, "seek first to understand, then to be understood."

As school districts move into actively seeking more stakeholder involvement and a deeper recognition that there are no simple solutions to problems inherent within complex, systematic organizations, we find that communication is even more essential. Communication must be interactive so that stakeholders' ideas and concerns can actively impact the direction an organization is taking. We can no longer afford the efficient, but highly ineffective, one-way communication by memoranda or newsletters. Written surveys, although attempting to elicit a two-way conversation, are highly impersonal and easy to disregard. Each of us in an organization must actively seek out communication with one another on the micro- and macrolevels in a highly humanistic manner.

Open communication, as it might be applied at a school site, brings back the metaphor of the gymnastics team versus the basketball team presented earlier. Traditionally, teachers have performed behind the doors of their classroom. They occasionally interacted with one another in the faculty lounge or at brief staff meetings. They spoke to parents at yearly back-to-school nights or when a student was having a problem. Their contact with support personnel was primarily task related—"The room is too hot." "Would you copy this ditto for me?" "What's for lunch?" Their interaction with administrators was primarily supervisor-supervisee. Everyone completed his or her individual task independently to support the teacher, whose responsibility was to make learning happen among a roomful of students throughout the instructional day. There was little or no time or desire to meet in cross-functional teams to nurture openness and trust, discuss visions for the future, or create innovations.

The process of transforming organizations is beginning to look different. Teams of cross-functional stakeholders are realizing that to achieve high performance they must know, trust, and rely on one another interdependently. Like a basketball team, they must communicate so that each can depend on the other to be in the correct position to make the big play.

Interpersonal communication behaviors can make or break the environment of trust and openness necessary for a group to transform into a high-performance team. An example of communication within a low-performing team would be a group of individuals who are constantly competing for "airtime," interrupting one another, having side conversations, participating in off-task behaviors as another group member is speaking, and making facial expressions or gestures indicating disagreement or ridicule.

An example of a high-performing team's communication would be a group of individuals who spend most of their energy respectfully listening to one another and seeking to understand different perspectives. There is a great deal of questioning for clarity and probing for more information. An acknowledgment of passion for a topic is not uncommon, and all issues are shared in a respectfully candid manner that honors fellow teammates' intellect and self-esteem.

Forms of Communication

Traditional forms of communication are, for example,

- I need to be heard.
- I need to criticize.
- My agenda must prevail.
- I must do many things quickly.

Transformed forms of communication are, for example,

- We need to listen.
- We need to provide honest feedback.
- Our agenda must be addressed.
- We must accomplish first things first.

There are numerous techniques, tools, and activities that can help a team develop a communication culture based on mutual respect, openness, and honesty. Some basic tenets to remember are the following:

- Ensure that each member of the team has a chance to be heard.
- Develop a shared knowledge base.
- Go slow to go fast.
- Listen with respect.

Summary

Through the development of a culture that honors and respects the roles that all its workers play and the contributions they make in enabling an organization realize its mission, an organization may transform itself into a high-performing quality system.

In the creation of this culture, openness, honesty, trust, and respect must be reflected in the organization's values, beliefs, and behaviors. Conflict must be encouraged and be focused on quality processes that identify core problems, seek data and knowledge, create and test hypotheses, and take action to institute change in an ongoing manner.

The organization must focus on systems development and not on inspection of the individual. Barriers to communication must be breached among all stakeholders in the organization, those external to the system as well as those who are internal. Continuous learning, professional growth, and organizational development must be sustained throughout the life of the organization. These all become essential quality premises in the leverage point of relationships.

Key Terms and Concepts

Dependence. An action, an idea, or a concept where a person or group acts in a needy, unempowered manner with others and their environment.

Group. When more than two people assemble for a purpose.

Independence. An action, an idea, or a concept where a person or a group acts in isolation from others and the environment.

Interdependence. An action, an idea, or a concept where a team is aware of its environment and stakeholders and seeks to collaboratively interact with both.

Organizational culture. The societal environment developed through the behaviors of people as they interact both formally and informally.

Synergy. A crucial habit one must master in order to be truly interdependent with others; the whole is greater than the sum of its parts.

Team. A group that has transformed into an interdependent entity that conducts its business and manages conflict in an environment of openness, honesty, trust, and respect.

Transformation. A change so complete that the new form developed from the change is uniquely different from what it was.

References

Covey, S. R. (1989). *The 7 habits of highly effective people.* New York: Simon & Schuster.
Deming, W. E. (1982). *Out of the crisis.* Cambridge: MIT Press.

Deming, W. E. (1986). *Out of the crisis.* Cambridge: MIT Center for Advanced Engineering Study.

Deming, W. E. (1992, October). *Quality, productivity, and competitive position.* Paper presented at Four Day Quality Seminar, St. Louis, MO.

Downey, C. (1993, Spring). Breathing life into the mission. *Quality Network News,* p. 2.

Glaser, W. (1990). *The quality school.* New York: Harper & Row.

Goldaber, I. (1982). Informal discussions with Greeley Education Association and Greeley School District #6 during win/win negotiations facilitation, Greeley, CO.

Hunter, M. (1982). *Mastery teaching.* El Segundo, CA: TIP Publications.

Joiner, B. (1985). *Total quality leadership vs. management by results.* Madison, WI: Author.

Ouchi, W. (1981). *Theory x.* New York: Avon Books.

Sashkin, M., & Kiser, K. (1991). *Total quality management.* Seabrook, NY: Ducochon.

Scholtes, P. R. (1988). *The team handbook.* Madison, WI: Joiner.

Senge, P. (1990). *The fifth discipline.* New York: Doubleday.

✧ 5 ✧

Getting Started

This chapter will assist educators who are interested in implementing the quality premises in their school districts. The first section helps you determine if you want to begin the quality journey. The next session proposes events and time lines for initiating quality, followed by some do's and don'ts. Finally, the chapter discusses Deming's (1982) 14th point—do it.

Determining Whether to Begin

The most important decision we, as educational leaders, have is whether we should begin the quality journey. Many of us, when we first look at the ideas of quality, say, "Oh, we are doing it." The reality is that when one examines school systems for each of the 18 quality premises of this book, few are implementing very many of the premises. And no district studied by the authors is implementing the premises in a total integrated way—in a sophisticated way. Most school systems have some type of mission, but that mission is often not alive and well in the system. Many of the employees do not see how they fit into the mission, and many see themselves as the customers of the organization.

With respect to benchmarks, few school systems are on a continuous improvement journey in all of the benchmarks in the educational best-practices arena. Breakthroughs of major impact on increased student learning are few.

With respect to structure, most systems function in a fragmented, linear fashion both in their organizational structure and their day-to-day management. Integrated, interdependent structures occur on occasion but not as the rule. Being a data-oriented system is difficult because it means a major mental model change on the part of employees to be research oriented and to use the data as feedback to improve the system.

With regard to relationships, many school districts disregard the people part of our business. Such educators wonder why people do not embrace the new benchmarks. We can have purpose and structure, but if we do not realize that people are the implementers, we will fail in our endeavors to move an organization from a status quo perspective.

It is highly recommended that, before a school system begins a journey into the quality movement, the governing board, the administrators, the key teacher, and the support leaders study the movement in detail. Those organizations that study the ideas for at least 1 year have had higher success rates for moving quality ideas into their system. Read the literature, attend the workshops, and learn. Being a learner first is a critical attribute in deciding about quality.

Deming (1982) talks about profound knowledge coming from outside the system. He believes that most organizations are working about as well as the people inside know how. Going out of ourselves to learn more about our work is critical. So the first step is to be a learner about quality.

Joiner (1985) identifies five ideas regarding starting:

1. Provide for education, reeducation, and active leadership of top management.
2. Develop a 2-year strategy for starting and implementing a quality improvement philosophy.
3. Set up a network of coordination, guidance, and technical support of the leadership.
4. Ensure organizational culture supportive of quality leadership.
5. Provide training and education to all stakeholders (employees, parents, students).

Implementing TQM: Proposed Events and Time Lines

Are there some suggestions about how we begin to implement quality premises in our school systems? Most definitely, yes. Downey (1993) contends that efforts need to be parallel at times, but there are some starting points. Starting with purpose before structure is important. And while working on purpose, trust in relationships must be established. Focusing on the customer is a good start. Know who the customers are, direct and indirect, as well as internal and external, before mission and vision statements are generated.

Next, Downey (1993) proposes working on a shared mission and then a shared vision. If the district has a mission statement, it needs to be revisited with the emphasis on "shared" mission. A vision statement needs to be updated—at least every 2 years. Downey recommends that benchmarks of best practice in the educational arena be used to create this evolving vision. Part of creating a vision is the parallel effort of increasing all stakeholders' belief in continuous improvement. We need to use strategies to help individuals decide if they really want to have the school district do a better job—working on a commitment toward continuous improvement.

Initial improvements could come from "low-hanging fruit"— easily implemented changes. Downey (1993) suggests that we work first on improving customers' services with internal employee customers. If we start on employees, services and staff see the school district improving in these areas. We can then move our employees to refocus from themselves as customers to other customers—especially our students.

Modeling from senior officers is critical. Working first on creating an organizational structure that provides for an integrated, systemic, cross-functional approach is essential. We must model our beliefs at that level before others in the organization will believe.

Senge (1992) identifies several aspects of building a foundation for a new organizational approach. They can be used to create a sequence of areas on which to work. Yet it must be remembered that changing an organization in a systemic way means that several parallel efforts will occur. Senge categorizes the areas to work on into (a) philosophy, (b) attitudes and beliefs, (c) skills and capabilities, and (d) tools (1992). His list is found in Figure 5.1.

BUILDING A FOUNDATION FOR THE NEW ORGANIZATION

Philosophy—we need to be clear about

    Purpose
    Vision
    Values
    Sense of Place

Attitudes and Beliefs—we need to have willingness to experiment

    Genuine caring
    Commonalty of purpose
    Power of systemic structure (beyond blame)
    Commitment to the truth
    We can create our future

Skills and Capabilities

    Personal Vision
    Seeing interrelationships (systemic structures)
    Building commitment
    Surfacing assumptions
    Balancing inquiry and advocacy
    Dialogue

Tools (Artifacts)

    System archetypes
    Generic structures
    Management flight simulators
    Action inquiry maps

Figure 5.1

The Goal/QPC organization (1992) has identified 10 elements for implementation that they propose will take at least 3 years to put into place. Figure 5.2 provides an illustration of the sequence of the 10 elements.

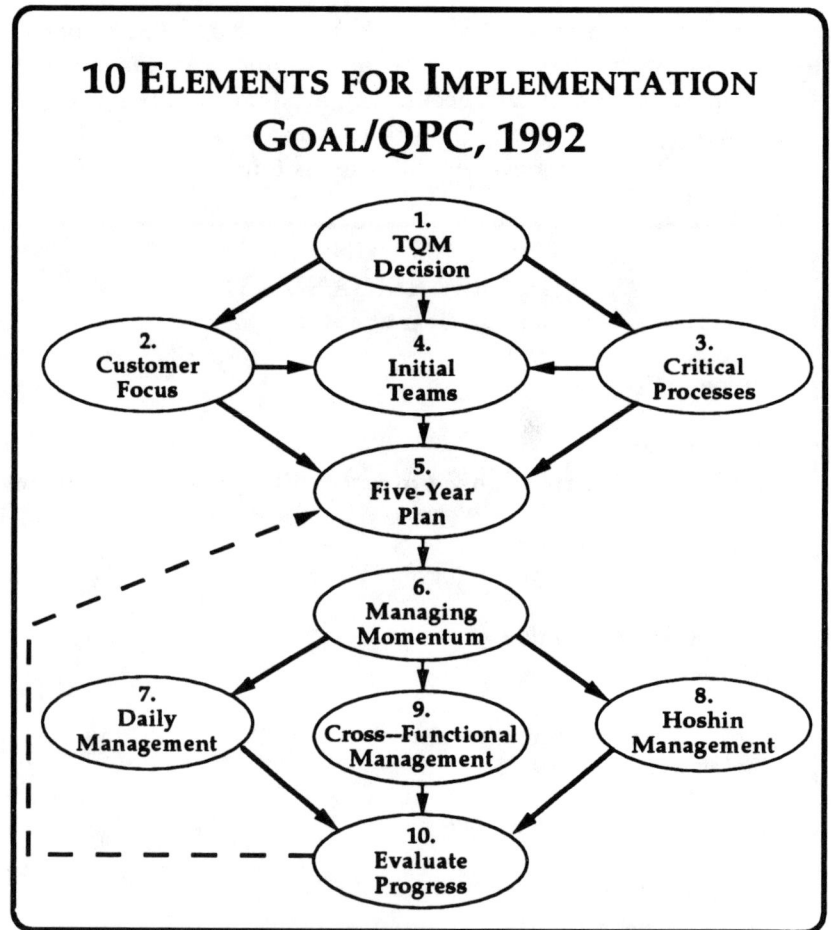

Figure 5.2

Love-Goodnight and Nakui (Goal/QPC, 1992) describe in detail the 10 elements. For each element, they also note which part of the PDCA (Plan—Do—Check—Act) cycle is involved. In fact, it is interesting to note that they propose a CAPD (check, act, plan, do) cycle for implementing quality premises. Figure 5.3 lists their ideas for each of the 10 elements with an educational interpretation for school districts.

(Text continued on page 118)

Goal/QPC's 10 Elements	Educational Implication
1. Check: Make the TQM Implementation Decision	*Make the TQE Implementation Decision*
• Analyze why TQM? Assess internal and external environments. (*Check*)	Are school system staff and community leadership willing to examine the district for improvement? Have board members, key community leaders, administrators, key teachers, and support staff spend much time exploring quality premises through readings and seminars.
• Achieve leadership consensus to initiate a TQM effort and establish a Senior Steering Group (SSG). (*Act*)	Achieve agreement among board members, superintendent, and other senior officers to implement quality premises. Do not establish a separate quality council but make this a major purpose of the superintendent's team or cabinet.
• Develop an education and training plan. (*Plan*)	Set in motion a staff development effort for all board members, staff, parents, and some older students.
• Educate and train personnel. (*Do*)	Implement the staff development program and provide an ongoing effort to ensure that new staff participate.
2. Act: Focus on Customers and Suppliers	*Focus on Internal and External Customers and Suppliers*
• Verify customer and supplier needs. (*Act*)	Same
• Design organizational structure for TQM. (*Plan*)	Develop a flattened, integrated, webbed organizational structure with a cross-functional team approach.
• Develop mission and vision statements. (*Do*)	Develop a shared mission (or revisit the mission) and develop a shared vision for 5 to 10 years.

Figure 5.3. Goal/QPC's 10 Elements and the Educational Implication (*Continued*)

113

3. *Plan: Initiate Daily Management-Defined and Evaluated Key Processes*	*Initiate Improvements in Daily Management-Defined and Evaluated Key Processes*
• Define and assess critical problems. (*Check*)	Define and assess critical problems/issues in the district.
• Identify and evaluate key processes to meet internal and external customer and supplier needs. (*Act*)	Identify and evaluate key processes to meet internal and external customer and supplier needs. Work on cross-functional issues as a system. Have departments/schools work on internal issues that are not cross-functional.
• Determine initial improvement projects (functional if possible). (*Plan*)	Same
• Evaluate, create, and improve processes as customer and supplier needs change. (*Do*)	Same
4. *Do: Establish Initial Teams (Daily Management Continued)*	*Establish Initial Teams (Daily Management Continued)*
• Organize initial teams and individuals to use the Quality Improvement Process (QIP) or a similar problem-solving methodology. (*Plan*)	Establish cross-functional teams and provide training on continuous improvement process using quality tools.
• Focus on critical problems and key processes. (*Do*)	Same
• Provide skills training, resources, and support for teams and individuals. (*Do*)	Monitor team progress in a supportive way and provide necessary resources, use an inclusion of stakeholder model for ongoing communication and input to the team.
• Evaluate daily management progress and feed analysis back to Element 2. (*Check*)	Same
• Communicate lessons learned to all levels and revise process where necessary. (*Act*)	Debrief process and communicate lessons learned to all those involved and revise process as needed.

Determine Hoshin (1-Year Plan for Annual Objectives)	
5. *Plan: Determine Hoshin (1-Year Plan for Annual Objectives)*	*Determine Hoshin (1-Year Plan for Annual Objectives)*
• Reanalyze internal and external environmental assessments and customer and supplier needs based on initial daily management progress. (*Check*)	Same
• Develop 3- to 5-year integrated business plan and annual objectives with targets in quality, cost, delivery, and morale. (*Act*)	Develop 3- to 5-year integrated school district long-range plan for major changes in the system and annual objectives with targets in best practices, budget, learner outcomes, and organizational climate.
• Design deployment strategy and determine means, control points, and checkpoints for top management targets. (*Plan*)	Same
• Plan for expanded daily management activities. (*Plan*)	
• Deploy *hoshin* to second and third management levels and initiate catch-ball activities. (*Do*)	Deploy *hoshin* to principal and supervisor levels and to grade level and department levels and initiate catch-ball activities.
6. *Do: Deploy Daily Management to All Levels*	*Deploy Daily Management to All Levels in the District*
• Plan for additional functional teams and initiate cross-functional teams. (*Plan*)	Same
• Schedule weekly or bimonthly meetings to review progress. (*Do*)	Schedule weekly or bimonthly meetings at the superintendent and divisional levels to review progress.
• Evaluate daily management progress and feed analysis back to Element 2. (*Check*)	Same
• Change daily management processes and procedures where necessary. (*Act*)	Same

Figure 5.3 Continued

	Initiate Hoshin Management Activities
7. Do: Initiate Hoshin Management Activities	
• Analyze catch-ball feedback and revise hoshin targets as necessary. (*Check*)	Same
• Develop means, control points, and checkpoints for second- and third-level management targets. (*Act*)	Develop means, control points, and checkpoints for divisional/principal-level management and grade and department level.
• Plan review system (Plan of Action and Milestones or POAM). (*Plan*)	Same
• Implement Plan of Action and Milestones (POAM). (*Do*)	Same
8. Check: Review Hoshin Progress (POAM)	*Review Hoshin Progress*
• Evaluate hoshin progress and feed analysis back to 3- to 5-year integrated business plan (Element 5). (*Check*)	Evaluate hoshin progress and feed analysis back to 3- to 5-year integrated school district long-range plan (Element 5).
• Revise targets, means, and hoshin management activities as necessary. (*Act*)	Same
• Design a benchmarking strategy. (*Plan*)	Same
• Initiate benchmarking activities. (*Do*)	Same
9. Act: Evaluate and Standardize TQM Progress	*Evaluate and Standardize TQM Progress*
• Evaluate progress (cultural transformation, support systems, results achieved through daily management, hoshin, and hoshin management) and standardize successful processes. (*Standardize*)	Same

• Account for successes and failures and feed analysis back to Element 2—repeat elements as necessary. (*Do*)	Same
• Evaluate Total Quality Management activities and plan for improvements in daily management, hoshin, and hoshin management. (*Check*)	Same
• Implement revised processes and policies. (*Act*)	Same
10. *Act: Establish Cross-Functional Management of Quality, Cost, Delivery, Morale* (QCDM)	*Establish Cross-Functional Management of Best-Practices Budget, Processes, and Organizational Climate*
• Evaluate TQM progress and determine readiness for cross-functional senior teams. (*Check*)	Same
• Establish senior-level teams for quality, cost, deliver, and morale (QCDM). (*Act*)	Establish senior-level teams for multiple targets.
• Design organizational structure and a review system to support senior-level teams. (*Plan*)	Design an integrated, webbed organizational structure and a review system to support senior-level teams.
• Integrate daily management, hoshin management, and cross-functional management, document result, and feed analysis back to Element 2. (*Do*)	Same

Figure 5.3. Continued

117

Love-Goodnight and Nakui (Goal/QPC, 1992) suggest that the 10 elements for implementing quality premises are at least a 3-year process. They depict the process as shown in Figure 5.4.

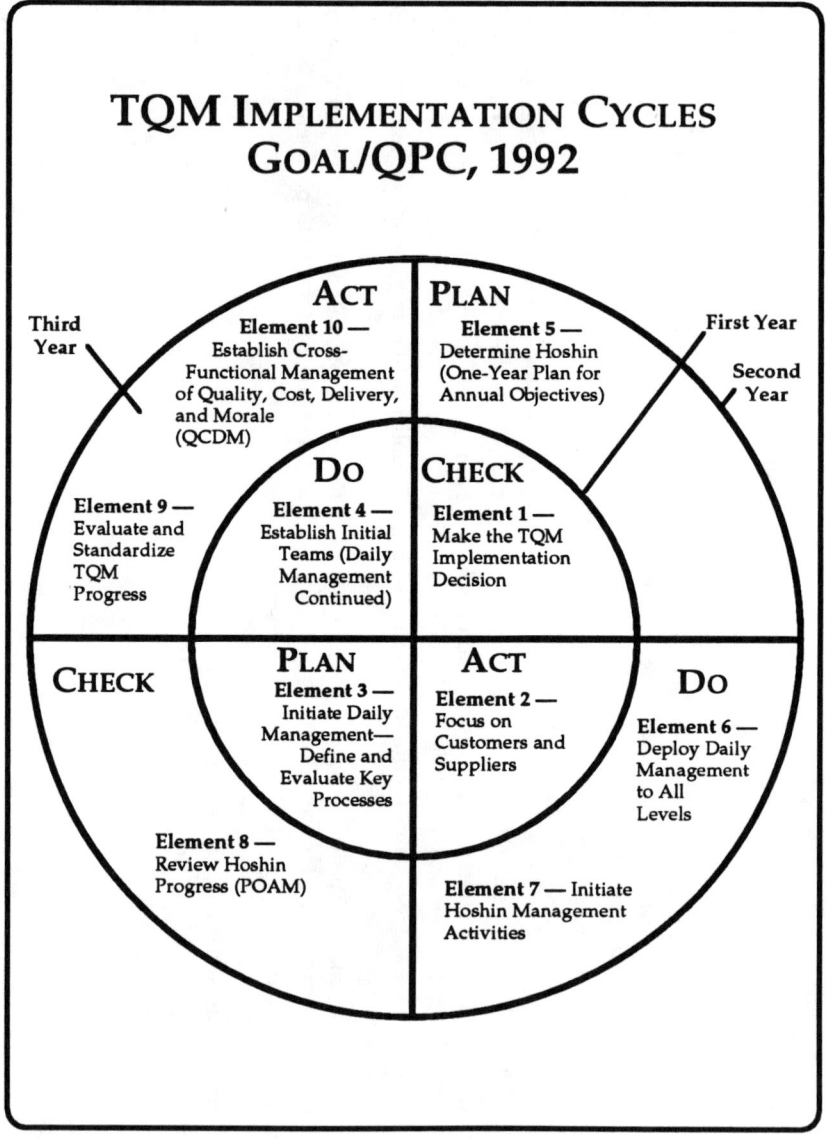

Figure 5.4

Specifying Some Do's and Don'ts in Implementing TQM

Many do's and don'ts for implementing quality come from practitioners and quality experts in the field (Joiner, 1985; Goal/QPC, 1992). First, let us look at the leverage point of purpose and some problems that can occur:

- A failure to identify all of the customers, internal and external, direct and indirect
- A failure to recognize that the student is the ultimate customer
- Selected services to provide that cannot be provided
- Not revisiting a mission, or not writing a mission, or a small number of people writing a mission with little input from employees and other stakeholders
- Assuming that if there is a mission it is understood by all
- Considering vision a waste of time
- A vision that is not tied to real quality problems or to an analysis of customer needs
- Board members and senior officers of the district who are indifferent to quality premises
- Reasons for initiating the quality movement that are unclear
- A scope of moving into quality that is limited to certain departments in the school rather than the entire school district
- Quality efforts that have not been structured and managed in such a way as to accomplish increased student learning—our business

Next, let us look at the leverage point of structure and some problems that can occur:

- Mistaking management for customer
- Quality premises unclear
- Not having a clear purpose for each meeting
- A lack of training for teams
- Teams failing to have commitment

- Cross-functional teams without parameters
- Being paralyzed by empowerment—not having the skills
- An implementation plan for quality that lacks measures, timetables, and responsibilities
- Quality tools not taught or used in improving the process
- Lots of design generated but not followed through
- Working only on daily management and a failure to move to mission/vision change
- Crisis and problems that are seen as an excuse not to do TQM rather than as a focus of TQM

Finally, let us look at the leverage point of interpersonal relationships and some problems that can occur:

- Employees who have not all bought into the quality premises
- Quality that is limited to teams only
- A failure to provide adequate training and opportunities to become committed to quality ideas
- Training that is limited to an awareness level only
- A mandated rather than an influence approach that is used to implement quality premises
- Unsuccessful risk taking and innovation that are used to blame people rather than as a celebration for trying something new

Probably the most important "do" is to remember that all three leverage points—purpose, structure, and interpersonal relationships—must be systemically influenced. If relationships are not at a trusting level, it is highly unlikely that any change of purpose or structure will have long-lasting effects in the school district.

Doing It—Deming's 14th point

Deming's (1982) last and most powerful point is to put everyone in the organization to work to accomplish the transformation—just do it. Certainly, there needs to be time for study, but soon there needs to be action, not just from the senior officials in the organization but from everyone. When everyone believes in the quality ideas, tremendous energy can be focused on increasing productivity in our school districts.

Senge (1992) provides a schema of a key mental shift in how we bring about that transformation (See Figure 5.5).

A KEY MENTAL SHIFT (SENGE)

AWAY FROM

Solve the problem.
Call in an Expert.
Form a task force.
Find a better technique.
Do it all now, right away.

TOWARD

Create the future.
Help each other learn.
Involve everybody.
Identify a valued purpose.
Do what is doable in
"reality time."

Figure 5.5

As we implement quality ideas in our school districts, it is important to remember what we know about change. Scholtes (1988) identifies several aspects of change as they relate to our quality endeavors:

- Keep in mind the "laws" of organizational change.
- Things are the way they are because they got that way.
- Unless things change, they are likely to remain the same.
- Change would be easy if it were not for all the people (a little tongue-in-cheek comment).
- People do not resist change, they resist being changed.
- Break down barriers.
- Identify informed networks.
- Build a critical mass.
- Treat change like a courtship.
- Anchor the change.

It has been suggested that we need a paradigm shift about change. We need to change to a continuous improvement framework. The traditional approach and the continuous improvement approach are shown in Figure 5.6.

A FRAMEWORK FOR CHANGE

The traditional approach to change is to
Step 1: Identify the problem.
Step 2: Find an expert.
Step 3: Tell everyone how to do it better.
Step 4: Overcome the resistance caused by steps 1, 2, and 3.

The continuous improvement approach to change is to
Step 1: Constantly look for the successes we are already having.
Step 2: Continually refocus on the ultimate objective.
Step 3: Continually search for what could be done to move even closer to the ultimate mission of the school system.

Figure 5.6

The question for us now is, do we begin? It means a long-term commitment to bringing about meaningful reform in our schools. But not doing it well could mean another decade where quality is lost to increased productivity. Just another fad—quality. Let us hope not. There are too many important quality premises to sacrifice another opportunity. Go for it.

Summary

This book has been written to serve as an overview of several major premises in the quality movement. Eighteen premises have been introduced and then placed into one of three leverage points—purpose, structure, and relationship—to create the Quality Fit Framework. We hope that it has served as a way of synthesizing for you many of the exciting ideas in the quality movement. Other books in this series provide more depth into several of the quality premises. Enjoy your quality journey.

Key Terms and Concepts

Continuous improvement approach. Three steps: constantly looking for current successes, continually refocusing on the ultimate objective, and continually searching for what could be done to move even closer to the ultimate mission.

Traditional change approach. Four steps: identify the problem, find an expert, tell everyone how to do it better, and overcome the resistance caused by the first three steps.

References

Deming, W. E. (1982). *Out of the crisis.* Cambridge: MIT Press.

Downey, C. (1993, Spring). Breathing life into the mission. *Quality Network News*, p. 2.

Goal/QPC. (1992, November). *Implementing TQM.* Paper presented at a 2-day pre-convention seminar, Boston, MA.

Joiner, B. (1985). *Total quality leadership vs. management by results.* Madison, WI: Author.

Scholtes, P. R. (1988). *The team handbook.* Madison, WI: Joiner.

Senge, P. M. (1992, February). Handouts and comments at the American Association of School Administrators Annual Convention, San Diego, CA.

✧ **6** ✧

Applying TQM in Education:
A Critical Analysis

American education has had a strong propensity to adopt educational innovations without first ensuring that there is a fit between
the problem and the solution or before research has supported the
innovations' merits (Slavin, 1989). Total Quality Management (TQM)
also has every appearance of being another fad. Quality is now the
"in" word; TQM continues to be represented as a magic elixir, and
the number of professional articles and books espousing the riches
to be gained through TQM continues its rapid growth.

The authors do not believe it is a cure-all or a panacea for all of
education's problems. We cannot imagine any one method or
strategy fulfilling the myriad of promises pronounced by the
self-selected proponents of TQM. Further, we believe that faddism
must be avoided. In this light, we use this chapter to address the
criticisms we are aware of and our opinions.

Examining the Criticisms of TQM in Education

Japan's Success With TQM Is Bound by Its Culture

Criticism of TQM is varied. One claim is that TQM is culture
bound. During a 4-day seminar on TQM, one critic decried Deming by stating that it is likely that TQM worked in Japan solely
because it fit the Japanese culture, ethics, and so on (Deming, 1992).

This criticism has been negated by the fact that TQM has also been used effectively in the United States and other countries.

Reducing Variation/Reducing People

Another major criticism of TQM is that Deming's focus on "reducing variation" is inhumane because current thinking strongly suggests that creativity and variation in people are needed and desirable (Fenwick English, personal communication, September 16, 1993). Reducing variation *in people* is a misinterpretation. The traditional interpretation of this "Tayloristic" notion is to make people robots to gain uniformity on the assembly line. This was not Taylor's intent. He was an early advocate of the belief that dictatorial position management is counterproductive and that owners and workers should cooperate to enhance the quality of the product *and* work life.

However, Taylor's notions about cooperative management were not only absent in the management ideology that followed, but they were misconstrued to mean the exact opposite. The net result was a reduction of variation between workers, low morale, re- duced creativity, and decreased quality of products. This is the point of English's criticism: Variation cannot be reduced without reducing people. This is a caution to educators to resist interpret- ing TQM as a manifestation of theory X. It is a criticism that may be reflected in practice, but does not have to be.

Book 4 in this series, *Creating Learning Places for Teachers, Too* (Frase & Conley, 1994) addresses the concern about reducing vari- ation or people, particularly teachers. The authors illustrate the theory and the techniques to be used to not only prevent this but to foster it. Teachers in TQE schools are not robots any more than workers in a TQM factory are. They are dynamic and questioning, ever attempting to improve the system and their professional skills.

TQE school administrators empower teachers to modify the system to achieve a high-quality state so that despite the wide variety of student characteristics, all students attain a high-quality education. The accent is on cooperation rather than competition. Further, TQE embodies applications of postindustrial practices such as transformational leadership (Burns, 1979), reflection (Schon, 1984), and learning organizations (Senge, 1990). However, it is important to recognize that one of Deming's points is to understand variation and then to constantly improve processes with that understanding.

Concerns About Competition and Metaphors

Alfie Kohn (1993, p. 59) expressed concern that applying the industrial model, with its focus on numbers, competition, customers, and buying and selling, not only reflects a warped view of education but contributes to the warping. Sztajin (1992) has expressed similar views. Specifically, their concern is that the use of industrial-based (e.g., TQM) metaphors will accelerate the tendency toward teaching by the numbers, for example, excessive competition among students for the highest achievement test scores. The authors agree that these concerns can be manifested in schools. However, they need not be, as illustrated in this series and in the work of schools using TQM concepts (Bonstingl, 1992; Johnson, 1993; Schmoker & Wilson, 1993).

Kohn (1993) also states that no educational literature on TQM has even remotely addressed learning or curriculum. This may have been true prior to English and Hill's (1994) book. Their work conceptualizes and integrates the best thoughts on curriculum and learning over the past 90 years.

Pallas and Neumann (1993) have questioned nine aspects of what they consider to be TQM assumptions and their applicability to higher education. They comment that the questions are also pertinent to the application of TQM in public education. The nine aspects in question are grouped into three categories: emphasis on tight coupling, assumptions regarding rationality, and reduction of variation. Each category is addressed in the following sections.

TQM's Emphasis on Tight Coupling

Pallas and Neumann (1993) contend that tight coupling, a strong linkage between an organization's vision and all actions within it, would prevent schools and colleges from "conducting education while simultaneously responding with credibility to the often conflicting or inappropriate demands of powerful external agents who require responses" (p. 22). Their claim is that loose coupling makes it possible for educational institutions to develop subsystems to respond to various demands.

In response, neither Deming (1986, 1992) nor TQM implies that only the chief administrative officer should make decisions. Rather, Deming (1992) is quite clear that everyone in an organization must participate in transforming it to one where all are involved in improving the work environment, the work processes, and the work product. Second, the critics imply that TQM is *bureaucratic* rationality or mechanical, rather than *substantial* rationality that is reflective and self-organizing (Morgan, 1986). In essence, they complain that TQM is goal directed and thereby overemphasizes "its concern with coherence, and . . . its attention to linear sequencing of thought and action." TQM does imply rationality and organization, but the authors know of no organization that has succeeded without designating goals and establishing plans to attain them. However, effective organizations do alter plans to keep on target. All members of a TQM team must see and know the global picture, actively participate in attaining the ends, and help formulate changes to ensure meeting the ends (Deming, 1993). This is clearly illustrated in Shewhart's Plan—Do—Study—Act (PDSA) cycle (see Deming, 1993).

The notion that substantial rationality implores everyone to follow their own leads and to do what they want anytime they want is nonsense, a near-perfect illustration of professorial fuzzy-headedness. Highly successful renegade companies such as Apple Computer Company are examples of the principles of rationality and loose coupling working in concert to attain success.

The issue of constancy of purpose, Deming's first of 14 points, is germane here. Many U.S. companies failed to stick to their areas of expertise in the 1970s and 1980s. They overdiversified and failed. A recent example is Westinghouse's ("Stake in 14 Hotels," 1993) action to sell 14 hotels to gain liquid capital in an attempt to stop massive financial losses. It was smart to sell them. It was foolish to acquire them in the first place. After all, what does Westinghouse know about hotels? The situation could have been avoided had they maintained greater constancy of purpose and stuck to their area of expertise.

With regard to education, it is possible that coupling should be tightened (Weich, 1982). This may be the most effective way to focus education on a task long enough to accomplish it, rather than changing goals on the political whims of ignorant critics and politicians—those in government and those in schools. Pallas and Neumann's (1993) extreme views of bureaucratic and substantial rationality appear to offer them the comfort of continuing to not only determine and implement the best way to get a job done but also to determine the job. No legislation offers individual teachers the authority or responsibility to determine the curriculum *and* the prescribed means for delivering it. Such a school would be anarchy and would accomplish little—think for example of the Summerhillian-type schools of the 1960s and 1970s, where the means became the ends and students learned little.

Questions About TQM's Assumptions Regarding Rationality

Pallas and Neumann (1993) claim that the rationality promised by TQM misconstrues the relationship between human thought and action, "expecting thought to produce action rather than the more likely reverse" (p. 25). This argument has come and gone repeatedly, without successfully demonstrating its claims in practice. In response, one has to ask the authors if they wait until they run out of gas before they fill up, or do they wait until they are out of breakfast cereal before they stock up? Are filling up and stocking up detrimental to people? We do not think so. It simply makes sense, and we wager the authors practice rationality at home. It is at work that they resent rationality. If it were their children in question, it is likely they would want the teacher to have a predetermined curriculum of some sort. This argument harkens back to the Rousseauian notion of *natural unfoldment,* where the teacher makes no assumptions about what children should know and instead waits for the children to unfold and to demonstrate their needs. Rousseau's ideas failed in Europe, and Dewey, a descendent, failed in the same quest in the United States in the 1920s. Dewey's followers failed again in the 1960s and 1970s. These arguments about rationality are old and tired. Further, they are self-serving and lack substance.

Questions About Reduction of Variation

Pallas and Neumann (1993) characterize reduction of variation incorrectly. They assume variability refers to differences in workers, that is, teachers. It does not. Deming (1992, 1993) clearly states that workers in every organization should be continually involved in making improvement in the work systems, expressly to achieve success and experience joy in work. This point, to constantly improve work systems, is made very clear in the red bead game that Deming employs in his 4-day seminars. In this game, workers are not allowed to communicate and are forced to work with a system that cannot possibly produce desired results, regardless of how hard employees work. Encouraging creativity and diversity for workers is a hallmark of TQM. Improving quality of learning is its aim.

Granted, no one instructional methodology works best for every teacher. TQM calls for groups of employees to continually examine the environment for ways to improve. The requirement to allow for and promote continuous learning is also clearly illustrated in the red bead game. It is echoed over and over again in TQM literature.

The remainder of the criticisms or questions are variations on the same themes. Pallas and Neumann (1993) conclude, "We do not expect our analysis to be terribly persuasive—not because of the lack of merit of our arguments, but because of the tenor of the times" (p. 37). The essences of their criticisms are cognitively misguided and philosophically deranged. Certainly, the tenor of the times will eschew acceptance and so will the merits of their criticisms. They claim one can only perceive TQM and its possibilities for education through their wide lenses. They claim that if TQM is viewed through other lenses it can only be seen as a panacea. That is quite self-aggrandizing; certainly there is room in education for more than one lens.

We know of no one who denies that education has room for improvement, and many agree that there is room for much improvement. Rejecting TQM on misapplied theoretical and philosophical principles is malpractice. Learning about it, finding in it that which can bring about improvements, and making adjustments along the way are the practices of professionals. To fully reject an idea that has already demonstrated benefits (Schmoker & Wilson, 1993) and falling back on only moderately successful practices replete with frailties is not wise. The Pallas and Neumann posture regarding TQM is a perfect misapplication of the reasoning by the King of Hearts in *Alice's Adventures in Wonderland* after reading the nonsensical poem of the White Rabbit: "If there is no meaning in it, that saves a world of trouble, you know, as we needn't try to find any" (Carroll, 1992, p. 102).

No reasonable leadership or management practice should be discredited based on whim. Likewise, no practice should be transferred "as is" from one company to another, one educational system to another, and certainly not from one country to another. TQM must be modified to accommodate the talents and the needs of people in the organization and its clients. The criticisms of TQM are theoretical. They will be proven or disproven in practice.

Key Terms and Concepts

Bureaucratic rationality. Rationality that is inhumane, for example, focuses on mechanics of the organization.

Competition and metaphors. A criticism, similar to reducing people, that using an industrial-based model such as TQM will accelerate teaching by the numbers and competition.

Culture bound. A criticism of TQM's applications to organizations in countries other than Japan, stating that the strategy can only work in Japan due to the unique features of the Japanese culture.

Rationality. The belief that productivity is dependent on goals and targets that become the focus for the organization's resources.

Reducing people. A criticism of TQM stating that one of its basic premises (reducing variation) is mechanistic and inhumane and can only result in reducing people from creative individuals who desire to do good work.

Reducing variation. Used in TQM literature to indicate the reduction of differences in processes and systems used to deliver a product as a means of improving its quality.

Substantial rationality. Rationality that is humane, for example, reflective and self-organizing.

Taylorism. Frequently used to describe management processes derived from theory X—the belief that workers are not internally motivated to do good work and must be coerced to do good work.

Tight coupling. Close alignment between the companies' mission, resource allocation, and efforts of all employees.

References

Bonstingl, J. (1992). The total quality classroom. *Educational Leadership, 6,* 66-70.

Burns, M. (1979). *Leadership.* New York: Simon & Schuster.

Carroll, L. (1992). *Alice's adventures in wonderland.* New York: TOR.

Deming, W. E. (1986). *Out of the crisis.* Cambridge: MIT Press.

Deming, W. E. (1992, October). *Quality, productivity, and competitive position.* Paper presented at Four Day Quality Seminar, St. Louis, MO.

Deming, W. E. (1993). *The new economics.* Cambridge: MIT Center for Advanced Engineering Study.

English, F., & Hill, J. C. (1994). *Total quality education: Transforming schools into learning places.* Thousand Oaks, CA: Corwin.

Frase, L., & Conley, S. C. (1994). *Creating learning places for teachers, too.* Thousand Oaks, CA: Corwin.

Johnson, J. (1993). Total quality management in education. Oregon School Study Council, *36,* 1-45.

Kohn, A. (1993). Turning learning into a business: Concerns about total quality. *Educational Leadership, 51*(1), 58-61.

Morgan, G. (1986). *Images of organization.* Beverly Hills, CA: Sage.

Pallas, A., & Neumann, A. (1993, March). *Blinded by the light: The applicability of total quality management to educational organizations.* Paper presented at the meeting of the American Educational Research Association, Atlanta, GA.

Schmoker, M., & Wilson, R. (1993). *Total quality education: Professionalization of schools.* Bloomington, IL: Phi Delta Kappan.

Schon, D. A. (1984). Leadership as reflection in action. In T. J. Sergiovanni & J. E. Corbally (Eds.), *Leadership and organizational culture* (pp. 36-63). Urbana: University of Illinois Press.

Senge, P. (1990). *The fifth discipline: The art and practice of learning organizations.* New York: Doubleday.

Slavin, R. (1989, June). PET & the pendulum: Faddism in Education. *Education Index, 70,* 752-758.

Stake in 14 hotels is sold to pay down bank debt. (1993, July 10). *New York Times,* Business Day Sec., p. 19.

Sztajin, P. (1992, November). A matter of metaphors. *Educational Leadership, 50,* pp. 35-37.

Weich, K. (1982). Administering education in loosely coupled schools. *Phi Delta Kappan, 27*(2), 673-676.

Planning and Troubleshooting Guide

Total Quality Education/Management (TQE/TQM)